"Take a Knee is like oɪ ninety-days workout viueos, only this is for your soul. There's more than thirty days' worth of training in this book. You'll want to start again from the beginning until you've mastered each exercise. The sooner you Take a Knee, the sooner life makes sense. And when you do, it's gonna be 'Look out, world!'"

Bradie James,
Dallas Cowboys Linebacker,
Founder of Bradie James' Foundation 56, bradiejames.net

"Focus. Follow-through. These are elements critical to success in my game, and critical to all men in the game of life. John drives home each spiritual challenge with the wisdom and depth of a man who isn't willing to accept less than God's best in his life. This is a must-read for all men."

Justin Leonard,
Twelve-time PGA Tour Winner, justinleonard.com

"There's no fluff in Take a Knee! John doesn't pull any punches in this straightforward challenge to men. He keeps it real as he talks about the issues men face in their daily struggle to be men of God. Great insight, practical suggestions, and helpful encouragement packed into a small space. This is a slam dunk."

Pat Williams,
Orlando Magic Senior Vice President,
Author of Extreme Focus, patwilliamsmotivate.com

WINNING PLAYS FOR THE GAME OF LIFE

DR. JOHN TOLSON

TAKE A KNEE

Take a Knee is a registered trademark of The Tolson Group.

To contact, email info@thetolsongroup.com.

Cover and Interior Design: Roark Design Co., www.roarkdesignco.com

Published by Franklin Green Publishing, LLC

Printed in the United States of America

ISBN 978-1-936487-27-1

DEDICATION

Take a Knee is dedicated to Jim Williams,
my friend for nearly 37 years.
Your wisdom, encouragement and
coconut cream pies will always be treasured.

I will always remember what Jim frequently says,
"God's hand is in everything!"

CONTENTS

ACKNOWLEDGEMENTS

Anyone who has ever written a book understands (unless they have a gigantic ego) that no one can pull it off alone. That is definitely true of me.

This book comes out of years of working with college and professional athletic teams. It has been my privilege to walk with and speak into the lives of many players, coaches and sports organizations. My goal has always been to motivate, inspire and instruct athletes to be great in their sport but more importantly to be a winner in life. These thoughts have also been communicated with business and professional leaders around the country as well.

Here are a few people who have played a special role in what you are about to read:

Jim Williams   **Richard Ellis**
Punky Tolson   **Rob Wilson**
Mark Gaither   **Scott Shuford**
Michelle Earney   **Stacy Smith**
Sarah Pearson   **Steve Van Amburgh**

My gratitude also extends to the teams who have opened their doors to these messages:

The Houston Rockets

The Houston Oilers (now Texans)

The Houston Astros

The University of Central Florida, Knights Football

The Orlando Magic

The Dallas Cowboys,
and various other college and professional teams.

Without the tireless efforts of the team members around me, Michelle Earney and Sarah Pearson, this book would not be in your hands. From beginning to end they used their God-given gifts to help produce Take a Knee. I would especially like to thank the Board of Directors of The Tolson Group for their support, encouragement and friendship.

Last, but certainly not least, the most special recognition goes to my family. I am tremendously grateful to two important women in my life. It is rare that a man should be blessed with a loving wife and wonderful marriage, but the Lord has blessed me twice. My first wife, Ruth Anne, to whom I was married for 30 years, went to be with the Lord in 1999. With her love, encouragement and blessing I was able to be away from home many weekends as I traveled with various sports teams while she stayed home with our two young children.

ACKNOWLEDGEMENTS

Likewise, my wife of 13 years, Punky, has not only encouraged me in my work and travels with the teams, but also took on my teaching commitments in my absence. I could not have served as a team chaplain without the blessing and support of these two great ladies.

To my daughter Christin and son Luke, I love you both and thank you for being the first young players to shape and influence the coach and father I am today.

To Christin's husband Joe, you are a faithful follower of Jesus, terrific husband and wonderful dad! And finally, to my three crazy and fun granddaughters, Adrien, Adair, and Josie - your "Bubba" loves you!

I am grateful to God for His relentless pursuit of us, and pray the Lord will use this book to start a movement by igniting in every reader a deeper love and commitment to Jesus Christ.

Warmly in Him,

John F. Tolson

FOREWORD
BY TONY ROMO

In professional sports, winning is everything.

That's not a criticism; it's a fact. Like a lot of other professions, the economy of football is simple. You keep getting paid as long as you can promise greater success than the guy standing behind you. This is a good thing that makes good players become great. Coaches demand nothing less than your best with each and every performance.

After signing with the Dallas Cowboys I earned a spot as the third string quarterback for the team. I knew that if I wanted to be a starter in the NFL, I was going to have to show the coaches that I was improving. Looking back, my faith and work ethic that my father and mother instilled in me helped me to find a way to get better. Initially, as with all professions I struggled in the beginning to learn my craft. Eventually, I began to learn how to be an NFL quarterback.

Looking back my faith helped me to let go. I surrendered all of my pressures to God. I was progressing because I felt an easiness come over me. I would give my best and leave the rest in God's hands. According to John Wooden, the legendary coach of the UCLA Bruins, "Success is a peace of mind attained only through self-satisfaction in knowing you made the effort to do your best of which you are capable." I have come to understand that God not only wanted me to lead a football team but also to be the spiritual leader of my home, which includes my wife Candice and my son Hawkins.

"Fortunately, success in the spiritual life doesn't depend entirely upon me."

Success as the spiritual leader in my home means more to me than anything because it's bigger than me. Success or failure as God's man now affects two other people. Fortunately, success in the spiritual life doesn't depend entirely upon me. God said He would not leave us alone, but help us every step of the way. In my case, the Lord provided several great examples to follow, beginning with my own dad. In addition, I have a pastor, Matt Chandler, who provides teaching from the Bible. My father-in-law sets a strong pace as the spiritual leader of his home. David Shivers, a former chaplain with the Dallas Cowboys, has been a great influence. And, of course, there's Dr. John Tolson, whose book contains the kind of practical, biblical advice all men need if they hope to be successful spiritual leaders.

FOREWORD

Like other athletes who have learned from John, I can tell you he never sugar-coats the truth and his Bible teaching is always practical and useful. You won't hear any religious "power of positive thinking" nonsense coming from him; only wisdom from the Bible that he has put into practice himself. His insights get straight to the heart of the matter and his advice helps make sense out of life. He's straightforward and practical in person, and this book is no different.

What John has to say in *Take a Knee* won't always make you feel good. But don't let that stop you. Push through the pain. Follow through with the advice he offers and, like a good physical training program, you will begin to see results. Believe me, it's worth it. As you lead others—especially your family—you want to win, John Wooden style. You want peace of mind knowing you gave your best.

Tony Romo
NFL Quarterback for the Dallas Cowboys

INTRODUCTION

I *love* sports. I'm convinced God invented athletic competition just to admire His handiwork after creating humanity. Where else but in the competitor's arena can you see a more impressive display of human potential? Just think about the broad range of sports and the abilities they demand: speed, strength, agility, balance, concentration, dexterity, stamina. When you watch the Olympic Games—a concentrated showcase of human ability—you'll also see that excellence comes in many shapes and sizes. What an incredible testament to the creativity of our Maker!

But that's just one reason I love sports. They also give us the opportunity to *learn*. Competition brings out the very best in humanity and exposes the very worst. A gracious winner inspires me to behave humbly. A resentful loser cautions me to hold my temper—and my tongue—when things don't go my way. A crowd cheering for a fallen runner who completes a race assures me that *how* we compete impacts people more profoundly than scoring a first-place win. A bad call by an official reminds me that life is not always fair, but you can't let injustice stand in the way of victory. The lessons I learned through sports as a kid stay with me to this day, and watching athletes keeps those timeless principles fresh.

Of the many kinds of athletic contests, I like team sports the most. I like the added dimension of cooperation. Like life, having to work with others complicates the simplicity of individual effort. God didn't create people to live in isolation, and in sports, no individual—regardless of how gifted he or she is—can win without teammates. Talented athletes must add to their physical abilities a sophisticated set of relational skills, and nowhere is this more evident than in professional sports. That need is where I come in.

For more than thirty years, it has been my privilege to work among some of the world's most gifted athletes, helping them strengthen three crucial relationships: their relationship with self, their relationships with others, and their relationship with God. It has been my experience that when any one of those three relationships goes sour, the whole team suffers. Coaches and team owners know this as well; so, they invite men like me to serve as Team Chaplains. After years of playing high school and collegiate team athletics, the Lord combined my own love for sports and my passion for impacting athletes for Christ, and placed me inside the locker rooms of NBA, MLB and NFL teams. I serve these organizations by conducting a weekly chapel service, offering a short devotional in the locker room before each game, leading staff Bible studies, and meeting with players for one-on-one personal coaching in life.

INTRODUCTION

The book you hold in your hands was inspired by the messages I've shared with professional teams before the beginning of each game. My goal is to drive the team to *think* and *feel* something, and to *motivate them to action*. I hope to do the same with you as you take on a very different kind of challenge. As you read these thirty-one daily thoughts, preferably in the morning—*before* taking the field!—try to imagine yourself in the locker room. Close your eyes and breathe in the aromas of competition; let the smells of acrylic, leather, cloth tape, and liniment mix in your nostrils. Listen to the clack of cleats, the squeak of rubber soles, and the pounding of pads as players get psyched up for battle. Feel your teammates lock arms with you as they form a circle and I say, "Take a knee."

We have just a few moments together before the challenges of life try to keep you from your goals, so pay close attention. Be fully present and give your complete attention to this time. Then, I invite you to join me in a short prayer. Just like I do with teams on game day, we close with three *amens*, each one louder than the last. Then, I trust you will have something worthy of consideration all day long.

Are you ready? Then, circle up and take a knee.

FINISHING WELL

THE PLAYBOOK

I have fought the good fight, I have finished the race, I have kept the faith. Now there is in store for me the crown of righteousness, which the Lord, the righteous Judge, will award to me on that day—and not only to me, but also to all who have longed for his appearing. (2 Timothy 4:7–8 NIV84)

THE GAME PLAN

"Let's take a knee."

In 1968, during the Mexico City Olympic marathon, the lead runner crossed the finish line, posting a time of 2:20:26. In the next half-hour, forty-three runners completed the 26.2 miles. Far behind them on the course, a Tanzanian runner fell, opening a gash on his knee and severely injuring the joint. But, John Stephen Akhwari wouldn't quit. After a hastily applied bandage stopped the bleeding, he trudged on. As the sun gave way to dusk and the stadium crowd slowly dwindled, he trotted, hobbled, walked, and limped toward the finish line.

Finally, a little more than an hour after the first-place finisher, Akhwari walked through the tunnel leading into the stadium. With a final burst of determination, he awkwardly trotted around the track toward his goal—finishing dead last. It should be noted, however, that seventeen other runners never finished at all. The next day, when asked why he refused to quit, he replied, "My country did not send me 11,000 kilometers to start the race. They sent me 11,000 kilometers to finish the race."

World-class athletes who do not possess all of those

qualities won't last long in the elite ranks of professional sports or Olympic competition. The seventeen men who started the race with Akhwari were the best competitors their countries had to offer, men of proven ability to endure discouragement, overcome setbacks, disregard injury, and ignore fatigue. Still, they quit before completing the course. What kept Akhwari going when his colleagues stopped?

Akhwari maintained a mindset that I frequently see in the most extraordinary athletes: a recognition that they do not compete merely for themselves. They enter the competition as individuals, but they never persevere alone. They may encounter a multitude of reasons to quit, but they have many more reasons to persevere: the people who believe in them, support them, rely upon them, or look up to them.

Very few of us will ever reach the upper echelon of athletic competition, yet I can say this for every person reading these words: *You do not run merely for yourself.* There are people in your life who depend upon your perseverance, your determination to do what is right, your commitment to finishing what you have started. That may be a project, a career, a financial obligation, a promise, or a relationship. Furthermore, whether you believe this or not, you are someone's *hero*. Your commitment to finishing what you have started will impact the lives of certain people—and you know who they are—in ways you may not have considered.

When your difficulties become unbearable, think about them. Then, finish. Don't quit.

TALKING TO THE COACH

Dear Lord,

Sometimes the trials of life are too much to handle,

and I admit the temptation to take the easy way out,

to leave my responsibilities for others to fulfill,

to turn my back on the difficulties that take the fun out of life,

to quit the race and do my own thing.

When I am weak, Lord, fill me with Your strength.

When I want to quit, Lord, push me forward.

Help me to focus on the good of others,

especially those who count on me most,

and let my impact on them keep me in the race

all the way to the finish.

In Jesus' name I pray,

AMEN. AMEN. **AMEN!**

GAME TIME

1. What obligation or commitment are you most tempted to quit? Who would be most negatively impacted if you were to give up? What consequences would you face if you choose to quit?

2. Considering Hebrews 10:35-36, if you see your commitment through to the conclusion, how will your perseverance positively impact this person (or people)?

3. Enlist the help of a trusted friend or advisor in your resolve to remain faithful to your commitment. When will you contact him or her?

THE INVISIBLE MAN

THE PLAYBOOK

[Jesus] sat down and called the twelve. And he said to them, "If anyone would be first, he must be last of all and servant of all." (Mark 9:35 ESV)

THE GAME PLAN

"Let's take a knee."

I have a friend who reminds me of Bruce Wayne (aka Batman). With a single phone call, he can reach virtually any political or corporate leader in the world. But he's not a politician, a celebrity, a financial heavyweight, or even a sports icon. Very much the opposite. This unassuming, humble man works quietly behind the scenes changing the world by influencing the hearts of world leaders. His name is Doug Coe, one of Time magazine's "25 Most Influential Evangelicals in America," a man they called "a stealth Billy Graham."[1] He's the Associate Director of "The Fellowship," whose mission is "to work with the leaders of many nations, and as their hearts are touched, the poor, the oppressed, the widows, and the youth of their country will be impacted in a positive manner."

One afternoon he gave me a profound piece of advice:

"John, you have to learn to be invisible."

"What do you mean?"

"Did Jesus have an office? Did He have a campaign manager? Did He advertise?"

"No."

"The point is this: Be low profile. It's not about you."

The words, "It's not about me," planted themselves deep in my soul and changed my life.

True leaders serve people, seeking their best interests and caring for their needs. Leaders aren't always popular; they may not always impress; in fact, they may never receive recognition. But because true leaders are motivated by loving concern for others rather than the desire for personal glory, they willingly pay the price of anonymity.

Think about it. Who's the most important player on a pro football team? Most would point to the quarterback, arguing that the game is in his hands. But without the protection of the offensive line, the most visible player on the team doesn't stand a chance.

The most important players are the guys who train day-in and day-out to make the team shine, regardless of their position or the recognition they receive. They become great by making others great.

Do you live to promote yourself? Or do you live to promote the name of Jesus Christ? Do you serve yourself? Or do you set aside your own comfort to serve others? Remember, you don't need a title to make a difference.

TALKING TO THE COACH

Dear Lord,

Thank you for the example of Jesus,

the humble servant of all.

Help me to promote You over myself,

teach me to put others first.

Make me comfortable with invisibility,

eager to serve behind the scenes.

When people see me,

may they see a great person only because I serve a magnificent God.

In Jesus' name I pray,

AMEN. **AMEN. AMEN!**

GAME TIME

1. Jesus challenged His disciples to be servants. What is one practical way you could meet this challenge today? Add it to your calendar to set a deadline and tell someone what you intend to do. Ask him or her to follow up with you later.

2. When is the last time you consciously placed someone else's success above your own? Did you expect a reward from God?

3. If you expect to be rewarded for serving others, have you really chosen to become invisible?

---

1 Time, "The 25 Most Influential Evangelicals in America," Feb. 7, 2005.

THE RULE OF ANYWAY

THE PLAYBOOK

Let us not become weary in doing good, for at the proper time we will reap a harvest if we do not give up. Therefore, as we have opportunity, let us do good to all people, especially to those who belong to the family of believers. (Galatians 6:9–10 NIV84)

THE GAME PLAN

"Let's take a knee."

Talent is a minimum standard for professional athletes. Lots of talented young men wash out of the NFL, the NBA, and MLB because they don't have *heart*. Champions keep going when difficulties make others quit. Champions learn to play through pain. Champions trust their training and continue to execute the game plan rather than panic. With that in mind, let me challenge you to gut through the difficulties of life as you apply the "rule of anyway."

People are unreasonable, illogical, and self-centered. *Love them anyway.*

If you are successful, you will attract false friends and true enemies. *Succeed anyway.*

The good you do today will be forgotten tomorrow. *Do good anyway.*

Honesty and frankness make you vulnerable. *Be transparent anyway.*

The biggest people with the biggest ideas can be shot

down by the smallest people with the smallest minds. *Think big anyway.*

What you spend years building could be destroyed overnight. *Build anyway.*

People in need often attack those offering help. *Help people anyway.*

Give the world the best you've got, and you'll get kicked in the teeth. *Give your best anyway.*[2]

TALKING TO THE COACH

Dear Lord,

Give me humility and grant me patience to serve You

when the rewards are few and far in between.

Give me courage and grant me strength to live for You

even as the world rewards evil.

Give me hope and grant me peace to trust You

while the world crumbles around me.

Give me joy and grant me confidence

as I love You when the world hates me.

In Jesus' name I pray,

AMEN. AMEN. **AMEN!**

takeakneebook.com

GAME TIME

1. If, in the future, the choice to do good might make you the least popular person in the room, what will you do?

2. What if the negative consequences involve more than mere embarrassment? What are you willing to endure for the sake of doing what is right?

3. What does your answer say about your trust in God? Discuss this with someone you trust within the next 48 hours. Go ahead and set up that appointment now.

---

2 Adapted from "The Paradoxical Commandments" by Dr. Kent M. Keith, paradoxicalcommandments.com

WINNING WITH CLASS

THE PLAYBOOK

For everyone who exalts himself will be humbled, and he who humbles himself will be exalted. (Luke 18:14b NIV84)

THE GAME PLAN

"Let's take a knee."

While aggression and confidence fuel some of the greatest players in the NFL, the truly great distinguish themselves through humility. For example, Chicago Bears running back, Walter Payton, crossed the goal line more times than most in his twelve-year career. Once he tucked away the ball, he either stutter-stepped around defenders or plowed over them to reach the end zone. But you never saw him showboating or belittling his opponents. Rather than flaunt success, he often handed the ball to a teammate or an official—a fitting illustration of humility.

Humility isn't low self-esteem. Humility isn't revealed in lack of effort or a reluctance to win. Humility doesn't require us to back away from competition. In fact, humility isn't even an attitude. Humility is a choice, a decision to regard another more important than self. In victory, humility gives dignity to those who have been defeated. A person is humble when he or she allows his ability to do the talking and then engages his mouth only to talk positively about others.

You will have an opportunity before this week has ended, and maybe even sooner. You will be presented with a choice. You can either exalt yourself in victory, or you can sing the praises of another. Be forewarned, however. Self-aggrandizement comes at the cost of humiliation later.

TALKING TO THE COACH

Dear Lord,

Help me to live with class,

to play with class,

to honor You in times of success,

and to thank You even in difficulty.

Help me see myself as You see me,

remembering that You care more about how I live

than whether I succeed or fail.

Nevertheless, help me to succeed,

and may my life bring encouragement to others

and glory to Your name.

In Jesus' name I pray,

AMEN. **AMEN. AMEN!**

GAME TIME

1. How does someone calling attention to his own successes shape your opinion of him?

2. Why do you think humility requires greater personal strength than boasting?

3. What is the best way to gain enough strength to be humble? (Hints: 1 Samuel 30:6; Psalm 18:20–29; Psalm 31:23–24) What are you going to do in the next twenty-four hours to gain this kind of strength?

THE FLAGMAN
OF OUR FAITH

THE PLAYBOOK

...Let us throw off everything that hinders and the sin that so easily entangles, and let us run with perseverance the race marked out for us. Let us fix our eyes on Jesus, the author and perfecter of our faith, who for the joy set before him endured the cross, scorning its shame, and sat down at the right hand of the throne of God. (Hebrews 12:1-2 NIV84)

THE GAME PLAN

"Let's take a knee."

As a fighter jet approaches an aircraft carrier to land, the flight deck looks like a postage stamp floating on an endless expanse of blue. Then, upon final approach, the landing runway becomes a moving target, bobbing, pitching, and rolling with the sea. Many pilots describe a carrier landing as a controlled crash. In the old days, before the advent of the lens optical landing system, the key to achieving a controlled crash instead of the other kind was to watch the flagman.

The flagman used handheld flags to direct the pilot's approach, precisely guiding his alignment and elevation. To get home in one piece, the pilot had to focus completely on the flagman and trust him completely. (You probably see where I'm going with this.)

The object of our focus determines our approach to life. If we choose to focus on money, position, possessions, applause, or other temporal things instead of "fixing our eyes on Jesus," the flagman of our faith, we'll end up in a million pieces scattered over the flight deck of life. Believe me, as a chaplain serving men surrounded by distractions, I've seen too many lives destroyed by focusing on the wrong object.

We have only one hope: focus completely on Christ, follow His instructions, and trust Him completely.

TALKING TO THE COACH

Dear Lord,

Help me to ignore distractions

against making Your will my focus.

Let me pursue what You value

above anything the earth admires.

And, Lord, help me to focus on the flagman of my faith;

Let me make Your Son my example,

and give me both wisdom and strength to follow Him.

In Jesus' name I pray,

AMEN. **AMEN. AMEN!**

GAME TIME

1. If someone were to review your spending and flip through your calendar, what would he say are your top three priorities?

2. What time or expense have you committed to learning about Christ's priorities? (See Matthew 22:36–40)

3. If Jesus is our flagman, what concrete change will you make to learn about Jesus and His priorities?

———————————————————

ATTITUDE DETERMINES ALTITUDE

THE PLAYBOOK

I press on toward the goal to win the prize for which God has called me heavenward in Christ Jesus. All of us who are mature should take such a view of things. And if on some point you think differently, that too God will make clear to you. Only let us live up to what we have already attained. (Philippians 3:14–16 NIV84)

THE GAME PLAN

"Let's take a knee."

When I served as the chaplain for the Houston Rockets, I had the privilege of walking alongside them through the 1981 season and into the NBA Finals. The Boston Celtics proved to be a formidable opponent, rising to take a 3-2 lead in the series.

Game six. Fourth quarter. Six minutes left. The Celtics struggled to score as Houston put up thirteen unanswered points. From my courtside seat, I caught a glimpse of Larry Bird's determined expression. He wasn't going down without a fight. I looked at the guy sitting next to me and said, "Watch Bird take over."

On the next possession for the Celtics, Bird kept the ball. *Swish*. Nothing but net.

Next time down the floor, he hit another three.

Before Houston could score again, he stole a pass, and put up three more points.

In moments, Boston won the game 102–91 to take the NBA Championship.

Larry Bird set his mind on getting the job done, and nothing was going to get in his way. He didn't let a recent string of team failures change his attitude.

I am convinced that attitude affects altitude. Larry Bird saw victory as his destiny and he played like a winner.

According to Paul the apostle, victory has been assured for all those in Christ. Not necessarily wealth, worldly success, achievement, or fame. Those things might come to you and they might not. That's not a part of God's promise. According to the Bible, those who trust in Christ have already gained victory over evil, sin, and death. It's just a matter of living out that victory today. So, despite any recent moral failures you may have had, victory is still yours. Now, let me challenge you to take on life like a winner.

TALKING TO THE COACH

Dear Lord,

Despite my failures of the past,

remind me that You have already secured the victory on my behalf.

Help me to make up my mind

and to approach future decisions with a winner's attitude.

Help me to play with passion,

to execute the basics well,

every down, every play, the entire game.

Lord, help me to live with the attitude

that victory is my destiny,

not because I deserve it,

but because You have promised it.

In Jesus' name I pray,

AMEN. **AMEN.** **AMEN!**

takeakneebook.com

GAME TIME

1. How have past moral tumbles affected your ability to face future temptation without falling?

2. Given your present attitude, how likely are you to fail in the immediate future?

3. If you were given proof that you would eventually conquer all temptations, how would you live differently today? What specific action will you take and when?

_____

CONSISTENCY IS KEY

THE PLAYBOOK

There should be a consistency that runs through us all. For Jesus doesn't change—yesterday, today, tomorrow, he's always totally himself. (Hebrews 13:8 MSG)

THE GAME PLAN

"Let's take a knee."

The animal kingdom is all about survival. Keep from being eaten so you can live to eat another day. God gave creatures the ability to cope with their ever-changing environments and some have developed amazing techniques to stay alive. One of the most intriguing is the chameleon. This little lizard has the ability to change his skin to match the color and pattern of any surface he walks across. If he crosses sand, he turns sandy brown. When he sits on a leaf, he's green. I've even seen a chameleon glow bright pink to match my neighbor's shutters.

As a survival technique, the ability to change one's appearance is impressive. As a character trait, I can't think of anything more cowardly or repulsive. Some people have the ability to blend into any crowd, able to hear the unspoken expectations of the most influential people and then present themselves in the most acceptable form. Among liberals, they're politically correct. Among conservatives, they're morally outraged. They carouse with the partiers and pray with the devout. Human chameleons cheer for the winning teams, agree with the majority opinions, stroke the right egos, and—I'm sad to say—they often go far in the world.

Jesus calls us to do the exact opposite. Rather than adapting to fit in with this world, He calls us to become more like Him, whom the world hated. Rather than blend into our environments, He calls us to remain consistently devoted to His way of thinking, speaking, and behaving. He commands us to be the same, in spite of where we happen to be and regardless of who might disapprove. Just as He is the same yesterday, today, and forever, He calls us to be consistent. It's a bad survival technique—He promised the world would hate His followers (John 17:14)—but as a character trait, consistency honors God.

TALKING TO THE COACH

Dear Lord,

The world rewards chameleons

and spews venom at those who proclaim Your truth.

The pressure to conform grows stronger

as my nation and my society drifts further from You.

I need Your unyielding strength to stand strong,

I need Your unreserved encouragement to stay courageous,

I need Your unwavering support to remain consistent.

Help me to trust You for survival

and as I seek You, may the world see Christ in me.

In Jesus' name I pray,

AMEN. **AMEN.** **AMEN!**

GAME TIME

1. In the recent past, have you taken the path of least resistance by denying your Christian identity in order to blend in with the crowd? If so, what did your conscience tell you?

2. What do you think will happen if others see your Christian ethic on display?

3. Jesus said the world will hate His followers; what are you willing to sacrifice to live consistently with your faith? When will you do this? Set a deadline and tell someone about your intentions.

BULLDOG FAITH

THE PLAYBOOK

...Pursue righteousness, godliness, faith, love, endurance and gentleness. Fight the good fight of the faith. Take hold of the eternal life to which you were called... (1 Timothy 6:11–12 NIV84)

THE GAME PLAN

"Let's take a knee."

Marines succeed in combat because they're driven by a mantra drilled into them from their first days in boot camp: "Improvise, adapt, and overcome." If a leader is taken out, the next-in-command takes his place. If a piece of equipment fails or a plan comes unraveled, they find another way to accomplish the objective. They begin each mission seeing success as a foregone conclusion, so quitting is never an option. It's no wonder the Marine Corps mascot is a bulldog!

By the time Timothy was appointed to lead the church in Ephesus by his mentor, Paul, he had learned how tough the Christian life can be. After all, Timothy had seen the apostle beaten with rods, flogged with a scourge, stoned and left for dead, shipwrecked no less than three times, and thrown in prison too many times to count. Still, Paul continued to brave the constant dangers of wilderness, robbers, hunger, thirst, and exposure, all for the sake of his objective: strong Christians leading strong churches (2 Corinthians 11:24–28).

When the demands of ministry overwhelmed Timothy, Paul wrote to him, urging the younger pastor to exercise what might be called "bulldog faith." He said, in effect, "Get tough. Expect opposition. When things go wrong, improvise, adapt, and Christ will overcome. Victory is assured, so quitting is not an option."

We are in a war against evil. In fact, you may have suffered some setbacks lately—falling to temptation and struggling with shame, beaten by misfortune and succumbing to discouragement—but I have good news. Christ has assured us that victory over evil is a foregone conclusion. You cannot be defeated unless you abandon the fight and flee the battle. You may be battered, bloodied, and bruised, but you are not beaten. Quitting isn't an option, so improvise, adapt, and Christ will overcome.

Be a bulldog in the faith.

TALKING TO THE COACH

Dear Lord,

Help me to see the victory You have already secured.

Help me to face the enemy with a winner's attitude.

Give me the courage to do what is right

even after I have chosen to do what is wrong.

Grant me a deep desire to honor You

even though I have dishonored myself.

Fill me with Your Holy Spirit,

chase away the shame of defeat,

and let Your confidence overcome my doubts.

Lift me from where I have fallen

and give me the resolve to rejoin the battle.

In Jesus' name I pray,

AMEN. AMEN. **AMEN!**

GAME TIME

1. The struggle to do what is right can be difficult. Have you been so discouraged you wanted to give up? If so, what was the cause?

2. Satan loves to keep discouraged people isolated; it dooms them to moral failure. Think of a Christian person who can be trusted to listen and offer honest feedback. Who is that person?

3. If you don't have an ongoing alliance with another Christian, when will you get one started? Add this to your to-do list and tell someone about your commitment.

TAKE THE BALL

THE PLAYBOOK

Be on guard. Stand firm in the faith. Be courageous. Be strong. And do everything with love. (1 Corinthians 16:13–14 NLT)

THE GAME PLAN

"Let's take a knee."

Two West Coast college football teams faced off in a frenzied stadium, packed to the brim with 100,000 screaming fans. As the clock counted down, the home team took possession for the final drive of regulation time. Down by two points, they needed just a few yards to put them in field goal range.

As the team huddled, the coach sent in a play calling for the star running back, Leroy, to take the ball.

The quarterback called a passing play, the pocket collapsed, and he was dropped for a loss.

Again, the coach called for a Leroy to carry the ball.

Next play, the quarterback ran a play-action, faked the handoff to Leroy, and hit the receiver between the numbers for a two-yard gain. Not enough.

Finally, the coach abandoned any attempt at surprise and began screaming from the sideline, "Give Leroy the ball!"

Another passing play. A blitz. Another sack. Fourth and long. The coach called for a timeout.

The coach composed himself and said to the quarterback, "This is it. Last chance to score. A field goal is out of the question; our passing offense is getting us nowhere; we have to go for it all. Give Leroy the ball. Do you hear me?"

The quarterback looked the coach in the eye. "I can't. Leroy said he doesn't want the ball!"

The character of a person isn't revealed by success or failure; it shines when the pressure's on, when the game is on the line, when the outcome of a crisis hangs in the balance. Truly great people are willing to take the ball, even when the odds are stacked against them, and they give their best effort no matter what the outcome. They do what they must, they give all they have, and they leave the results in God's hands.

Facing a crisis right now? Take the ball. God will honor your commitment, win or lose.

TALKING TO THE COACH

Dear Lord,
Give me greatness of character, so that
when the pressure is on,
when the outcome is unsure,
when the risk of criticism looms large,
when called to shoulder responsibility,
I will not hesitate to commit myself
and do with honor what must be done.
I call upon Your strength
and I do all for the glory of Your name.
In Jesus' name I pray,

AMEN. **AMEN. AMEN!**

GAME TIME

1. Life is full of challenges for which we do not feel equipped to handle. What challenge do you now face that you privately hope will go away?

2. Many men and women share a common failing: When we don't know what to do, we do nothing at all. What responsibility have you been avoiding or delaying?

3. If at all possible, set a deadline for taking the first step (you know what it is), and communicate it to someone you respect. Have this person hold you accountable to get it done.

MAKE THE MOST OF NOW

THE PLAYBOOK

Be wise in the way you act toward outsiders; make the most of every opportunity. Let your conversation be always full of grace, seasoned with salt, so that you may know how to answer everyone. (Colossians 4:5–6 NIV84)

THE GAME PLAN

"Let's take a knee."

In 2007, sophomore quarterback Tim Tebow won the Heisman Trophy. In 2008, he led the Florida Gators to their second National Championship in three years. That victory gave the college junior a rare the opportunity to skip his last year of school and become a top pick in the upcoming NFL draft. Conventional wisdom said, "Seize the day! You could be injured as a college senior and lose your opportunity forever." Big money and a promising professional career hung in the balance.

One Saturday, he discussed the opportunity with his family and his coach; everyone leaned toward entering the draft. Then, Tim's aunt spoke up. "Tim," she said, "you've got one more year to play college football. Every camera in the nation is on you. Don't miss this opportunity to make an impact for Christ."

Tim had made no secret of his strong faith. Each week, he painted a Bible verse in white on his eye black—a practice forbidden in the NFL. As the cameras focused in on his face during the 2009 season, the entire television audience saw a verse reference he found particularly meaningful that week.

During the 2008 season championship game (on January 8, 2009), he wore John 3:16: "For God so loved the world that he gave his one and only Son, that whoever believes in him shall not perish but have eternal life" (NIV84).

The next season, while pounding the Troy Trojans, he painted Mark 8:36: "What good is it for a man to gain the whole world, yet forfeit his soul?" (NIV84).

Prophetically, his cheeks read, "John 16:33" during a disappointing defeat against Alabama: "I have told you these things, so that in me you may have peace. In this world you will have trouble. But take heart! I have overcome the world" (NIV84).

During the 2010 Sugar Bowl, Ephesians 2:8–10: "It is by grace you have been saved, through faith—and this is not from yourselves, it is the gift of God—not by works, so that no one can boast. For we are God's workmanship, created in Christ Jesus to do good works, which God prepared in advance for us to do" (NIV84).

And when he struggled through the Senior Bowl, his face reassured everyone with James 1:2–4: "Consider it pure joy, my brothers, whenever you face trials of many kinds, because you know that the testing of your faith develops perseverance. Perseverance must finish its work so that you may be mature and complete, not lacking anything" (NIV84).

Each week, Google searches for "Tim Tebow" and the Bible verse spiked dramatically.

In a remarkable step of faith, Tim placed his commitment to Jesus Christ over everything else, and he made the most of his opportunity in the spotlight to honor his Savior.

Don't miss the opportunity to honor Christ in whatever you do today. In big decisions and small, make the most of *now*.

TALKING TO THE COACH

Dear Lord,

Thank you for the opportunity to honor Jesus Christ.

May I live today and every day for You.

Help me remember what is truly important:

a life devoted to You above all;

gifts, talents, abilities, and advantages

that bring glory to You and not myself;

and the promise that my deepest desires

are found in advancing Your agenda above my own.

Give me the courage to choose Your will,

and to do things Your way above all.

In Jesus' name I pray,

AMEN. **AMEN. AMEN!**

GAME TIME

1. Think of a time you had to choose between a shortcut to glory and bringing honor to God. What was at risk? What did you choose? How did it turn out?

2. How often do you face the choice between instant gratification and delayed reward? What do you normally choose? What does this say about your faith in God?

3. Did you know that faith itself can be a gift from God? (Mark 9:23–24; Luke 17:5). Take time now to ask for what you lack: confidence in His ability or willingness to support you.

THOU SHALT NOT SWEAT IT

THE PLAYBOOK

Therefore I tell you, do not worry about your life, what you will eat or drink; or about your body, what you will wear. Is not life more important than food, and the body more important than clothes? But seek first his kingdom and his righteousness, and all these things will be given to you as well. Therefore do not worry about tomorrow, for tomorrow will worry about itself. Each day has enough trouble of its own. (Matthew 6:25, 33–34 NIV84)

THE GAME PLAN

"Let's take a knee."

Worry is a killer. When we worry, we act as though the things we fear have become a reality. When we worry, we actually make dreaded situations an emotional reality when they haven't even happened—and may never happen. In my experience, ninety percent of the things we worry about never come to pass anyway!

Worry occurs when we put our emotional energy into fighting something that hasn't yet occurred. And, if we're not careful, that wasted time and energy will keep us from being the best we can be—as a husband, father, friend, businessman, mentor, athlete, or coach. Worry pulls us down, steals our joy, undermines our confidence, diverts our energy, and impedes our success. We begin to focus far too much on what might happen instead of dealing with reality.

Jesus warned His followers about worry and issued a command. Let's call it The Eleventh Commandment: "Thou shalt not sweat it."

Let me challenge you to do one of the hardest things known to man. Refuse to spend any time thinking

takeakneebook.com

about the things you can't control. Commit those things to prayer. Instead, work and focus on those things you can control. Identify the activities that show the greatest promise of producing good results and focus on executing those tasks. Champions don't sweat the small stuff; they set their minds on what they must do instead of fretting over what might happen.

TALKING TO THE COACH

Dear Lord,

Help me to commit the things I cannot control to Your sovereign care.

Help me to identify the things You have given as my responsibility,

and give me the strength to execute them well.

Grant me the faith to set aside worry and to trust You completely.

In Jesus' name I pray,

AMEN. AMEN. **AMEN!**

GAME TIME

1. Identify at least one matter over which you have no control and causes you stress.

2. Each time that issue comes to mind, give it to the Lord to resolve in His time and in His way.

3. If you have a trustworthy Christian friend, ask him or her to pray on your behalf. When will you do it?

takeakneebook.com

LIVING ABOVE OUR CIRCUMSTANCES

THE PLAYBOOK

But when he asks, he must believe and not doubt, because he who doubts is like a wave of the sea, blown and tossed by the wind. (James 1:6 NIV84)

THE GAME PLAN

"Let's take a knee."

I asked a friend of mine, "Man, how are you doing?"

He said, "Well, under the circumstances, I'm doing okay."

"What are you doing under there?" I asked.

Too often, we live our lives under our circumstances, thinking we're trapped by the things that happen to us. We even allow our circumstances to determine whether we'll be happy or frustrated. When life goes smoothly, if we have everything we want, if we're able to stay ahead of our troubles, if we're treated fairly, then happiness comes easily. But when circumstances turn against us, if progress becomes an uphill climb, if income can't keep up with expenses, if justice turns upside down, happiness flutters off with the slightest breeze.

The apostle James called us out for living this way, instructing us to avoid being "driven and tossed by the wind." He challenges us to ask some tough questions. Who is our master? Circumstances or Jesus Christ? To what do we look for our happiness? Under whose control are we? Under God or "under the circumstances?"

I challenge you today—even as I confront my own conscience right now—choose this day which master you will serve. (See Joshua 24:15).

TALKING TO THE COACH

Dear Lord,

Free me from the dictatorship of my circumstances.

Fill me with divine calm as promised by Christ, who said

"My peace I give you. I do not give to you as the world gives.

Do not let your hearts be troubled and do not be afraid" (John 14:27 NIV84).

Free me to live according to Your promises.

Free me to overcome the world by trusting in You,

rather than succumb to the whims of circumstances.

Help me to find my happiness in the unchanging reality of who You are,

rather than be tossed with every shifting wind or rolling wave of circumstance.

In Jesus' name I pray,

AMEN. AMEN. **AMEN!**

GAME TIME

1. What recent circumstance beyond your control have you allowed to determine your mood?

2. How has your frame of mind affected those closest to you—your wife, children, friends, coworkers, employees?

3. If Jesus really is "Lord," how should that influence your perspective on the circumstances of life? What is one specific action you can take to help keep your perspective in sync with God's, and when will you get it done?

IF YOU GOT IT, *DON'T* FLAUNT IT

THE PLAYBOOK
Pride goes before destruction, a haughty spirit before a fall.
(Proverbs 16:18 NIV84)

THE GAME PLAN

"Let's take a knee."

Denny Holzbauer is a ten-degree black belt and six-time world champion kickboxer. And he's learned some incredible lessons from his career in the ring. One, in particular, caught my attention.

He tells the story about preparing for a match and watching the bout right before his. The first fighter strode out of the locker room in a flashy outfit with the house speakers blaring "Eye of the Tiger." He jumped on the ropes, raised his hands in anticipated victory, and turned a flip onto the canvas. According to Denny, martial artists don't typically behave like pro wrestlers. They stretch a little, shake out the tension, and start the fight. Showboating is considered disrespectful to the other fighter and shameful to your school.

The second boxer walked confidently to the ring from the locker room. He stepped inside, nodded to the first boxer, and then prepared to fight. Not long after the bell rang, Mr. Showboat lay face-up on the canvas, the victim of a one-punch knockout.

takeakneebook.com

If you've got it, you don't need to flaunt it. If you have talent, if you've worked hard, if you're prepared, then you have good reason to be confident. Just get the job done and let your results do the talking.

TALKING TO THE COACH

Dear Lord,

Help me to remember that all my abilities and skills come from You.

Help me to see myself as You see me,

a person worthy of dignity

yet still in need of Your grace.

Teach me to carry my confidence with humility.

Encourage me to do everything with excellence

with a heart full of gratitude for Your support.

May I do all for the sake of Your glory,

and for the honor of Your Son.

In Jesus' name I pray,

AMEN. **AMEN.** **AMEN!**

GAME TIME

1. What gift, talent, ability, or advantage do you have that many other people do not?

2. How much do you think you derive your self-worth from your unique advantages?

3. Do you think God is impressed? What do you think makes a man great in the eyes of God? Ask some of those closest to you to answer these questions based on their observation of you. Set a goal for at least three people in the next three days.

IN IT FOR THE LONG-HAUL

THE PLAYBOOK

Therefore, since we are surrounded by such a huge crowd of witnesses to the life of faith, let us strip off every weight that slows us down, especially the sin that so easily trips us up. And let us run with endurance the race God has set before us. We do this by keeping our eyes on Jesus, the champion who initiates and perfects our faith. Because of the joy awaiting him, he endured the cross, disregarding its shame. Now he is seated in the place of honor beside God's throne. Think of all the hostility he endured from sinful people; then you won't become weary and give up. (Hebrews 12:1–3 NLT)

THE GAME PLAN

"Let's take a knee."

I once had a buddy named Chris who gave new meaning to the word "endurance." Skinny as a rail and passionate about running, he could flat-out run—fast and far. I learned a thing or two about real endurance one day while running in my neighborhood. Chris came up behind me and started jogging by my side. Itching for some competition, I said, "Chris, do you see that sign up there?" The sign was about 150 yards away. "Let's race!"

We took off, and I actually did pretty well. But when we got to the sign, I slowed to a walk, gasping for air and totally spent. Chris breezed a couple of turns around me, and said, "Well, come on. Let's go!"

"What . . . *(gasp)* . . . do you . . . *(wheeze)* . . . mean?"

"John, I'm going another twenty miles."

"You're . . . *(huff)* . . . kidding!"

"No, I'm doing twenty-five or twenty-six miles today."

takeakneebook.com

Chris didn't train for sprints; he patiently and consistently prepared for long haul races. He understood the two indispensable strategies in long-distance competitions. First, train your heart muscle for endurance. Second, in cross-country courses, you can't see the finish line, so keep your eye on the lead runner and never let him out of your sight.

The writer of Hebrews calls us to cultivate a "long-haul" perspective. If life is a race, it's not a 100-yard dash; it's a cross-country feat of endurance. And the lead runner is Jesus Christ. To succeed, we must eliminate anything that slows us down, we must run with endurance, and—most crucial of all—we must keep our eyes on Christ. In a practical sense, that means learning who He is and doing as He did while on earth.

What kind of race are you running? What's your strategy for the long haul?

TALKING TO THE COACH

Dear Lord,

Help me to see life as it is:

a long-distance endurance challenge.

Challenge me to throw off anything that creates drag,

and inspire me to run with determination.

Teach me to keep my eyes on Your Son,

the perfect lead runner.

Help me to discover His character

and to imitate His behavior.

Constantly remind me that a great reward

waits for those who complete the course,

and give me the strength to run well.

In Jesus' name I pray,

AMEN. AMEN. **AMEN!**

takeakneebook.com

GAME TIME

1. How much time do you devote to your favorite pastime?

2. Recreation is a necessary part of life, but it's nothing compared to your spiritual health. Do you set aside as much time to building a strong spirit?

3. Using your calendar, set aside daily and weekly time to work on your spiritual health. Divide that time between two activities: 1) daily learning about Jesus Christ and, 2) weekly engaging in acts of service (feeding the hungry, volunteering for a charity, introducing others to Jesus, etc.) Share your plan with someone who will hold you accountable to follow-though.

GREAT EXPECTATIONS

THE PLAYBOOK

The words of a man's mouth are deep waters, but the fountain of wisdom is a bubbling brook. A fool's mouth is his undoing, and his lips are a snare to his soul. From the fruit of his mouth a man's stomach is filled; with the harvest from his lips he is satisfied. The tongue has the power of life and death, and those who love it will eat its fruit.
(Proverbs 18:4, 7, 20–21 NIV84

THE GAME PLAN

"Let's take a knee."

The World Heavyweight Champion fighter, Mohammed Ali, used to say, "I am the greatest! I'm the greatest of all time!" In fact, he composed and then recited long poems about his skills in the ring. Who can forget, "Float like a butterfly, sting like a bee"? Looking back on his career and reviewing his stats, it appears he saw back then what we see now. Ali was, arguably, the greatest.

By contrast, a young prisoner in a Texas jailhouse muttered, "Dad said that one day, I'd end up behind bars. I guess I didn't let him down."

I'm not suggesting we start bragging like Ali, and I'm not advocating a "name it, claim it" thinking. Still, words have a profound influence on who we see when we look in the mirror and that, in turn, affects who we become. Our words can have life-changing effects on others as well. That's because words, both positive and negative, have a way of becoming self-fulfilling prophecy. When we boldly declare truth and life, we clear a path to great accomplishments for ourselves and those we influence. Perhaps that's why Paul wrote to the church in Ephesus,

"Don't use foul or abusive language. Let everything you say be good and helpful, so that your words will be an encouragement to those who hear them" (Ephesians 4:29 NLT).

TALKING TO THE COACH

Dear Lord,

Let my speech become the overflow of a positive attitude.

While I commit to keeping my mouth shut

when I think of something negative to say,

and speaking up when encouraging words come to mind,

I know that willpower is not enough;

I need a thought transfusion.

I need You to change me from the inside out.

Create in me, Lord, a clean heart

and a positive spirit.

I ask in the name of Your Son, Jesus Christ,

AMEN. AMEN. **AMEN!**

GAME TIME

1. When you foul something up, what does the voice inside your head tell you? Is it typically positive and affirming or negative and degrading?

2. How often do you think of something positive to say about someone, or to someone, without actually saying it? What's holding you back?

3. How a person thinks has a huge impact on who he becomes and what he does. If you're serious about this, read Philippians 4:4–9 and then turn Paul's counsel into an action list. Call someone today to hold you accountable to working your action list.

takeakneebook.com

THE GOD WHO BELIEVES

THE PLAYBOOK

So, what do you think? With God on our side like this, how can we lose? If God didn't hesitate to put everything on the line for us, embracing our condition and exposing himself to the worst by sending his own Son, is there anything else he wouldn't gladly and freely do for us? And who would dare tangle with God by messing with one of God's chosen? Who would dare even to point a finger? The One who died for us—who was raised to life for us!—is in the presence of God at this very moment sticking up for us. None of this fazes us because Jesus loves us. (Romans 8:31–34, 37 MSG)

THE GAME PLAN

"Let's take a knee."

Early in the second quarter of the 1929 Rose Bowl, California Golden Bears team captain and center, Roy Riegels, suddenly saw the football bounce near his feet. Driven by instinct, he snatched up the ball on Georgia Tech's 30-yard line and started running. After a few steps, he spun to miss a pack of tacklers, broke free, and ran sixty-two yards . . . the wrong way! A teammate managed to catch him before he entered his own endzone, but the damage was done. A wave of Georgia Tech jerseys rolled over him one yard from his own goal line. A blocked punt on the next play gave Tech the safety and a two-point lead.

The crowd jeered. The opposing team taunted. His own teammates struggled to recover their morale. As the clock ticked down the final seconds of the half, Riegels trudged to the locker room, knowing that he would never live it down.

No one thought he'd return to play the second half, including Roy. As the team headed back to the field, Riegels didn't move. When Coach Nibs Price called for

Roy to join them, the dejected player said, "Coach, I can't do it. I've ruined you, I've ruined myself, I've ruined the University of California. I couldn't face that crowd to save my life."

Price replied, ""Roy, get up and go back out there—the game is only half over."

He did. He bolted onto the field, and put together the best half of his life. He went on to earn All-America honors and become team captain in his senior year. After graduating in 1931, Riegels coached high-school and college football, served during World War II as a major in the Army Air Corps, and then started his own agricultural chemicals business.

After a huge blunder in life, we might think Game Over! When failures tell us life isn't worth facing, God takes us by the shoulders and says, "Get up and go back out there—the game is only half over."

Believe it or not, God believes in you. He sees you in all your chaos, He gave His Son to redeem you, and He has pledged to carry you to victory. What's more, He does this knowing your future—successes, failures, and all.

TALKING TO THE COACH

Dear Lord,
Thank You.for believing in me so much
that You gave me Your Son.
You see my worth because You made me
in Your image and for Your glory,
and You have equipped me for great things
despite the constant drag of sin and error.
Now, Lord, help me to rise above past failures,
to expect great things from myself and others.
Fill me with strength and courage from You
to become examples of redemption.
In Jesus' name I pray,

AMEN. AMEN. **AMEN!**

GAME TIME

1. Think of a time when you've royally blown it—morally, in business, at home, with relationships. Since then, what have you shied away from doing as a result?

2. If you overcame your reservations, how did you do it? If not, what's holding you back?

3. On a 3 x 5 card or a sticky note, write down at least three areas in which God wants you to succeed. Post it where you will see it often for the next week. Each time you see the note, briefly ask God to equip you to succeed.

INDIVIDUAL DEMANDS

THE PLAYBOOK

…Live a life worthy of the calling you have received. Be completely humble and gentle; be patient, bearing with one another in love. Make every effort to keep the unity of the Spirit through the bond of peace. There is one body and one Spirit— just as you were called to one hope when you were called—one Lord, one faith, one baptism; one God and Father of all, who is over all and through all and in all. (Ephesians 4:1–6 NIV84)

THE GAME PLAN

"Let's take a knee."

Rowing may be the most demanding of all team sports, both physically and in terms of character. Individual rowers must maintain a precise balance between weight and strength. Each additional pound creates drag, so every ounce of body weight must produce more power than resistance. These athletes must also develop incredible cardio-vascular conditioning, enough to produce fifty strokes per minute for six minutes to cover a two-thousand-meter course faster than the competition. Yet for all their strength and conditioning, despite the demand for world-class athleticism, this is a terrible sport if you hope to earn MVP honors. As a team, they must row in perfect unison while maintaining impeccable balance and no individual can afford to slack off, neither in training nor in competition. That means each member of the team must turn in their best performance with no hope of individual recognition.

Whether you realize it or not, you are a member of a team. In fact, more than one. You have a team at home, a team at work, a team in your community, and undoubtedly a couple more you could name. These teams depend upon your individual performance—if you slack off, the whole team suffers—yet there's little chance of individual recognition.

Those who follow Christ are also part of a team. Paul the apostle described believers as members of a body with Christ as the head. When one part hurts, the whole body suffers. When one member slacks off, the whole body struggles. When one of us fails, everyone endures the sting of defeat.

If you're ever tempted to think that you don't matter, or if the thought ever crosses your mind that a small compromise here or little indulgence there won't hurt anyone, stop. Think again. When you give less than your best, even if no one else knows, every team you're on feels the loss.

Don't expect MVP honors, but never forget: You are invaluable to others.

TALKING TO THE COACH

Dear Lord,
Remind me today, and every day,
that I do not live in isolation.
Make me keenly aware of my impact on others.
Help me to turn in my best performance
not for individual recognition,
but for the success of all,
and for the glory of Jesus Christ.
Give me the wisdom to seek Your approval
over the applause of men.
In Jesus' name I pray,

AMEN. AMEN. **AMEN!**

GAME TIME

1. How many of the "teams" in your life are impacted by, and depend upon, your individual performance? (i.e. family, marriage, sports, work...)

2. Which of the above teams do you care about more than others, and why?

3. Considering 1 Corinthians 12:12-26, when you slack off or fail, what consequences must others bear as a result? Ask at least one person from each of the teams you care about the most to give honest feedback about your team-playing ability. Do this within the next forty-eight hours, and listen without interruption. Think about what they say, submit it to the Lord in prayer, and then ask Him how you should respond.

168 GIFTS PER WEEK

THE PLAYBOOK

The length of our days is seventy years—or eighty, if we have the strength; yet their span is but trouble and sorrow, for they quickly pass, and we fly away. (Psalm 90:10 NIV84)

THE GAME PLAN

"Let's take a knee."

Time is not a boomerang. It will never return to you. On the contrary, each hour of your life is an arrow, drawn from your quiver and released. The good it does depends upon your aim.

Every person in the world—rich or poor, powerful or helpless, wise or foolish—is given one hundred sixty-eight hours each week. Subtract eight hours a night for sleep and that leaves each of us one hundred twelve hours either to invest or to waste. One hundred twelve hours that will either return something of value or dissolve into nothing. I don't know about you, but I want to make the most of my time. So I schedule virtually every waking hour: family time, fun time, prop-it-up time, work time, think time, in-the-Word time.

I don't mean for life to become a perpetual motion machine, always moving, always producing. That's not wisdom; that's workaholism. I merely suggest that we should be conscious of every moment and whether it's put to good use. Rest is good. Fun is essential. Know how much you need to maintain health and sanity, and then schedule it. In fact, I would encourage you to try this little exercise. Take out a weekly calendar and jot down everything you typically do over the course of a week. Record everything from grooming in the morning, to time in traffic, time spent at work, time in front of the television, time with family, time eating dinner. Account for every block of fifteen minutes if you can. Then, add up the times.

If you're like most people, you can't account for about twenty hours. Twenty arrows shot randomly into the air.

Now, take that same weekly calendar and aim your arrows. Account for the time you do not control, like scheduled work hours. Then look at what's left. Block off sufficient time for what's important to you. Spouse. Children. Rest and relaxation. Spiritual enrichment. Exercise. Account for each priority, set aside time for it, and protect those appointments like you would a crucial business meeting.

Let us pray with the psalmist, "Teach us to number our days aright, that we may gain a heart of wisdom" (Psalm 90:12 NIV84).

TALKING TO THE COACH

Dear Lord,
My life is but a vapor,
here for a brief time and then gone.
Teach me to count each hour as a gift from You,
to be treasured as priceless,
managed like wealth,
and invested with wisdom.
And like all of Your gifts,
may I administer each hour unselfishly,
for the highest, greatest good of others
and the honor and glory of Your name.
In Jesus' name I pray,

AMEN. AMEN. **AMEN!**

takeakneebook.com

GAME TIME

1. Think of your top three priorities in life and list them, in order, on a piece of paper.

2. How many hours each week do you devote to each priority? Write the number beside each priority.

3. What wasted time can you recover and then devote to your top priorities? How will you do this?

BREEDING AND BROKENNESS

THE PLAYBOOK

We are his workmanship, created in Christ Jesus for good works, which God prepared beforehand, that we should walk in them. (Ephesians 2:10 ESV)

THE GAME PLAN

"Let's take a knee."

I grew up on a cattle ranch in Florida, where riding a horse was as common as driving a car. That's where I learned to love horses, one of God's most magnificent creatures. He put half a ton of muscle on four hooves, built the animal for speed, and placed within it a twitching need to run. Some of the world's most powerful and agile runners are Quarter Horses, yet they aren't controlled with a bit in the mouth like other breeds. All you need is a harness with two half-inch strips of leather. A Quarter Horse responds to the slightest touch on the neck with those reins; a simple "whoa" and a gentle tug brings the animal to a complete stop.

A great Quarter Horse is bred to run and trained to obey. Regardless of speed or strength, however, a horse that won't obey is useless, and in extreme cases, its will must be broken.

The Lord made you for good works, and He calls for obedience, but the choice is yours. You can do what you like and run where you wish, but you'll never

takeakneebook.com

achieve your full potential. Accepting Christ as Savior, on the other hand, includes a willingness to place all that you are and all that you have under His control. Only then can you accomplish what you were made to do. Only when taking direction from the Master can you fulfill your potential. Without obedience, however, you're like a horse without direction. *Useless.*

Read the prayer on the next page, offer it to the Lord, and then tell someone about the decision you've made.

TALKING TO THE COACH

Dear Lord,
I want You to control my life.
I want You to be my Master.
I want You to transform my mind
and direct my decisions.
All that I have is Yours.
Teach me to discern Your will
and give me the courage to do it.
I invite You to do whatever You must
to bend my will to Yours,
and to make me into the person You want.
In Jesus' name I pray,

AMEN. AMEN. **AMEN!**

takeakneebook.com

GAME TIME

1. Obedience isn't really obedience until your desires clash with His and you choose to set aside what you want to do as He commands. What area of your life are you reluctant to give over to God?

2. Disobedience is usually a lack of trust in the goodness of God. What do you fear will happen if you surrender your will to His?

3. Put your misgivings in the form of a prayer; tell them to God and ask for His help. Do it now and repeat it as they come to mind over the next couple of days.

BUSY BODIES

THE PLAYBOOK

Be very careful, then, how you live—not as unwise but as wise, making the most of every opportunity, because the days are evil. Therefore do not be foolish, but understand what the Lord's will is. (Ephesians 5:15–17 NIV84)

THE GAME PLAN

"Let's take a knee."

Here's a story that could describe any failing team anywhere. It's about four people named Everybody, Somebody, Anybody, and Nobody.

> There was an important job to be done and Everybody was asked to do it. Everybody was sure Somebody would do it. Anybody could have done it but Nobody did it. Somebody got angry about that because it was Everybody's job. Everybody thought Anybody could do it but Nobody realized that Everybody wouldn't do it. It ended up that Everybody blamed Somebody when Nobody did what Everybody could have done.[3]

That's funny! Until it happens in real life.

Having observed men and why they don't get things done—on the playing field and in life—one reason stands above them all: When a man isn't sure what to do, he does nothing at all. He's like a deer caught in the headlights of a speeding truck. He's paralyzed by a curious flaw in our nature. A man habitually shrinks from any task that reminds him of his inadequacy. He hates feeling unqualified, out-matched, overwhelmed, confused, or inept. So, rather than deal with the fact that he's not all-powerful, he avoids the offending responsibility.

King Solomon condemns inactivity with a sobering warning: "…The waywardness of the simple will kill them, and the complacency of fools will destroy them" (Proverbs 1:32 NIV84). The fact is, we cannot honor God if we put off our responsibilities. If we wait on someone else to step in, we are no less guilty of sin than if we deliberately did something wrong. When something needs doing, then doing nothing is a sin.

Fortunately, there's a way to overcome procrastination. First, be aware of when you have taken no action in a matter of great importance. Take notice when you know something should be done, and the consequences of delay could be grave, yet you put off doing anything about it. Most likely, you haven't acted because you're not sure what to do, or you know what to do and the task causes you to feel undeserving of respect. When you find yourself in that situation, let me encourage you to do something bold. Man-up and ask for help. No one expects you to be all-wise or all-powerful. *(No one except you!)* So, find someone with experience or training and buy him lunch. Or pay for an hour of his time. King Solomon, the world's wisest leader, wrote,

"For lack of guidance a nation falls, but many advisers make victory sure" (Proverbs 11:14 NIV84).

"Plans fail for lack of counsel, but with many advisers they succeed" (Proverbs 15:22 NIV84).

"For waging war you need guidance, and for victory many advisers" (Proverbs 24:6 NIV84).

When it's foolish to do nothing, find wise counsel and do something.

TALKING TO THE COACH

Dear Lord,

Forgive my complacency;

forgive my disobedience.

Help me to overcome my foolish inaction.

Lead me to find wise counsel,

and wisely overcome the challenge I now face.

Fill me with Your Holy Spirit,

push aside all traces of pride,

lift me higher than my self-reliance,

cast out any insecurity or distrust,

and prompt me to grasp a helping hand.

In Jesus' name I pray,

AMEN. AMEN. **AMEN!**

GAME TIME

1. What have you been putting off that needs your attention?

2. What about that task subtly suggests you're less than the person you think you are?

3. Who can help you get this responsibility done, and when will you make the call?

---

3 Adapted from the poem "Everybody, Anybody, Somebody, and Nobody" by Charles Osgood.

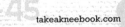

takeakneebook.com

ONE MORE ROUND

THE PLAYBOOK

…We also rejoice in our sufferings, because we know that suffering produces perseverance; perseverance, character; and character, hope. And hope does not disappoint us, because God has poured out his love into our hearts by the Holy Spirit, whom he has given us. (Romans 5:3–5 NIV84)

THE GAME PLAN

"Let's take a knee."

James J. "Gentleman Jim" Corbett came to be known as the father of modern boxing because of his scientific approach and technical innovation. In the late 1800s, boxing was one step above bare-knuckle brawling. Tiny leather mitts covered the fighter's hands. No boxing commissions regulated the sport or protected the fighters. No limit on rounds—boxers fought until one couldn't continue. But Corbett discovered that technique could overcome brute strength.

Corbett also earned a reputation for determination. As fighters say today, "There wasn't any quit in him." No matter how many times he was hit, regardless of how many times he was dropped to the canvas, and in spite of fatigue or pain, he refused to leave the ring with his opponent still standing. In his most memorable fight, Corbett faced Peter "Black Prince" Jackson, a fellow boxing instructor from San Francisco. On May 21, 1891, the two men battled for sixty-one rounds, one of the longest boxing matches recorded in those days. The California Athletic Club finally declared the match a "no contest" and all bets were off because club officials doubted either exhausted man could win.

I read a quotation from him that changed my life. He said,

> Fight one more round. When your feet are
> so tired that you have to shuffle back to the
> center of the ring, fight one more round.
> When your arms are so tired that you can
> hardly lift your hands to come on guard, fight
> one more round. When your nose is bleeding
> and your eyes are black and you are so tired
> you wish your opponent would crack you one
> on the jaw and put you to sleep, fight one
> more round—remembering that the man
> who always fights one more round is never
> whipped.[3]

All right, let's be honest. Life is a lot like a sixty-one
round fight. I don't mean to say that life is all hard
knocks and pain. If it is, then you're doing something
wrong! But life does bring hardship. There will never
be a time this side of heaven when you can say, "Whew,
no more difficulties; smooth sailing from here." The
pleasure of living will be punctuated by devastating
blows. And in the depths of pain and suffering, faith
becomes stretched to its limits. That's when trust in the
Lord gets reduced to trusting him one more day, doing
the next thing next, getting through one more day . . .
fighting one more round.

If that's where you are right now, let me join my voice with Paul's in a solemn promise. This will pass. You will emerge from this time a better person. The blood will dry, the bruises will heal, your strength will return, and you will look back on these days with an understanding of many things. Even if you're engaged in a fight for your life and you should succumb to death, God will turn this evil into unimaginable good, for all eternity.

Until the Lord, Himself, takes you to be with Him, fight one more round.

TALKING TO THE COACH

Dear Lord,

I have accepted Your truth as certainty,

You are good to those who cling to You.

But I admit there are times when my trust in You falters,

I see the unrighteous and arrogant succeed,

I see evil run roughshod over the innocent,

misery and heartache overtake the weary,

while unbelievers deny You exist and mock my faith.

I confess that, sometimes, giving up looks appealing,

but what hope do I have besides You?

Therefore, I choose to enter Your sanctuary,

I will join with other believers in worship of You,

and there, I will hear Your Word,

and take courage from Your promises,

and, with my brothers and sisters, be filled with strength

to fight one more round.

I submit my unbelief to You.

In Jesus' name I pray,

AMEN. AMEN. **AMEN!**

GAME TIME

1. If you are enduring a particularly difficult struggle, what do you fear most?

2. If you haven't already, enlist the help of a wiser, Christian man or woman to join their voice to yours in regular prayer.

3. If, on the other hand, you are fortunate enough to be free of crisis right now, someone you know is in the fight of their life. Find that person. Offer to meet with them regularly for prayer. When will you do it?

---

3 *Wisdom Well Said*, Charles Francis, ed. (El Prado, NM: Levine Mesa Press, 2009), 107.

EYE ON THE PRIZE

THE PLAYBOOK

When Christ, who is your life, appears, then you also will appear with him in glory. Put to death, therefore, whatever belongs to your earthly nature: sexual immorality, impurity, lust, evil desires and greed, which is idolatry.
(Colossians. 3:4–5 NIV84)

THE GAME PLAN

"Let's take a knee."

In 1940, British Prime Minister, Winston Churchill, refused to sign an armistice with Nazi Germany as a means of avoiding conflict with Hitler. He criticized neighboring countries for their appeasement, saying, "Each one hopes that if he feeds the crocodile enough, it will eat him last. All of them hope that the storm will pass before their turn comes to be devoured."[5] After ten months of air attacks by the German Luftwaffe, and intense fighting by the British, the "Battle of Britain" handed Hitler his first defeat.

In 1941, the British Bulldog returned to his old school to deliver a commencement speech. Churchill positioned his five-foot-seven-inch, two-hundred-twenty-pound frame behind the podium and scanned the eyes of the young men of Harrow School. In his speech, he said,

> Surely from this period of ten months this is the lesson: never give in, never give in, never, never, never, never—in nothing, great or small, large or petty—never give in except to convictions of honour and good sense. Never

yield to force; never yield to the apparently overwhelming might of the enemy.[6]

Winston Churchill understood his enemy and he kept his eyes on the goal: *victory!*

It's true, we are engaged in an all-out assault by Satan, whose battle plan is to distract you with nonessentials, to demoralize you with accusations of failure and worthlessness, to derail you with temptations, and to dishearten you through intimidation. He wants you to forget the victory Jesus Christ has secured for us. He wants you to give in; he wants you to get out of the fight. Just think of how many people Satan will have harmed if he can convince you to quit.

To echo Churchill, let me encourage you, "Never give in, never give in, never, never, never, never—in nothing, great or small, large or petty—never give in except to convictions of honor and good sense."

TALKING TO THE COACH

Dear Lord,

Thank You for never giving up on me,

for never turning away.

Protect me from the Evil One.

When Satan whispers his accusations,

prompt me to seek the truth of Your Word.

When I'm ready to give in,

send a comrade-in-arms to hold me accountable.

When I'm pulled down by memories of failure,

lift me up with visions of Your victory.

Because You are faithful to me,

I now commit to You,

I will never give in,

in nothing, great or small, large or petty.

Because You stand by me,

I will stand with You,

until the day Christ appears.

In Jesus' name I pray,

AMEN. AMEN. **AMEN!**

GAME TIME

1. In terms of your own struggles to remain morally upright, what does it mean to "give in?"

2. When do you feel most inclined to give in, and who will be harmed if you do?

3. Who can you call during these times for some moral support? If you don't have a trustworthy friend you can call, seek someone out and make arrangements to meet together.

---

5 Winston Churchill in his broadcast of 20 January 1940, quoted in *Winston Churchill and Emory Reves: Correspondence, 1937-1964* (Austin, Tex.: University of Texas Press, 1997), 230.

6 Winston Churchill in his commencement speech at Harrow School, 29 October 1941, quoted in *Never Give In!: The Best of Winston Churchill* (New York: Hyperion, 2003), 307.

THE WONDER OF WEAKNESS

THE PLAYBOOK

God chose the foolish things of the world to shame the wise;
God chose the weak things of the world to shame the strong.
(1 Corinthians 1:27 NIV84)

THE GAME PLAN

"Let's take a knee."

Young Billy was chosen to give the daily devotional at summer camp. It was his cabin's turn to give a devotional at the main assembly, and the junior high boys thought it would be funny to nominate Billy, who had cerebral palsy and no idea it was a prank. Honored and excited, he accepted.

It took much longer than normal for Billy to make his way up to the podium. His hands shook, his legs quivered, his face twisted, and his body writhed in random perpetual motion. As his peers snickered in the back row and the adults shifted uncomfortably, Billy struggled to utter just seven words: "Jesus . . . loves . . . me . . . and . . . I . . . love . . . Jesus."

The counselors had failed to interest the kids in Jesus, and even the professional baseball players, who had been recruited to inspire the kids, failed to make an impact. Instead, God used Billy's seven-word speech to trigger a revival. Tony Campolo, who tells this story, says that he routinely encounters missionaries and preachers who placed their trust in Jesus Christ that week at camp. What superstars couldn't pull off, God accomplished through a little boy—despite his physical limitations, with nothing to offer but his authentic love for Jesus.

God often uses our shortcomings to accomplish His purposes for one simple reason: In our weakness, His strength becomes most obvious. Are you willing to set aside your self-sufficiency, your pride, and your strength in order to let God work through you? Are you willing to depend fully on Him so that He might accomplish His purposes through you?

Or are you afraid of the "wonder of weakness"?

TALKING TO THE COACH

Dear Lord,

I want to be Yours,

the kind of person You want me to be,

to live in one-hundred-percent dependence upon You,

not twenty years in the future,

not when my career is over,

but today, right now.

Lord, I commit myself to You,

my strengths, my weaknesses, my all.

May Your will be done

in me and through me

for Your Glory above all.

In Jesus' name I pray,

AMEN. **AMEN. AMEN!**

GAME TIME

1. Everyone has weaknesses. In what way do you consider yourself inadequate, or incapable?

2. If it's true that God sometimes does His best work through our weaknesses, what will you do to allow Him to use yours?

3. Right now, offer your weakness as a gift to God and ask Him to either strengthen you or use that weakness to accomplish His goals.

SOARING INTO SIGNIFICANCE

THE PLAYBOOK

...[You] were taught... in accordance with the truth that is in Jesus. You were taught, with regard to your former way of life, to put off your old self, which is being corrupted by its deceitful desires; to be made new in the attitude of your minds; and to put on the new self, created to be like God in true righteousness and holiness. (Ephesians 4:21–24 NIV84)

THE GAME PLAN

"Let's take a knee."

In his book, The Pursuit of Excellence, Ted Engstrom tells the story of an Indian brave who found an eagle's egg and placed it in the nest of a prairie chicken. The baby eagle hatched along with the prairie chicks and began following their example. He scratched the dirt for seeds and insects; he clucked and crackled; he flew in a brief flurry of feathers no more than a few feet off of the ground. And, as the years passed, the odd little eagle grew very old.

One day, he saw a magnificent bird soaring high above, circling a cloudless sky with effortless majesty. "What a beautiful bird," said the earthbound eagle to a neighbor. "What is it?"

"That's an eagle; chief of the birds," the prairie chicken clucked. "But don't give him a second thought. You could never be like him."

The eagle never gave flying a second thought. Soaring to unimaginable heights had been his birthright, yet he spent his life pecking the ground for grubs like a prairie chicken. Eventually, he died, never realizing his true potential.

We are children of our Heavenly Father, made in His likeness to rule over the earth as His vice-regents. God created us for noble purposes, but Satan works overtime to keep us belly-down in the dust, too discouraged by shame to stand up and take responsibility for ourselves, our homes, and our world. He does this by tempting us to sin and then beating us down with our failures, saying, "You're such a disappointment to God, why even try to be good?"

The truth is, Satan has no power except the power of deception. The truth is, sin has no power over the Christian except the power we give it. The truth is, those who have claimed God's promise of salvation through His Son have received a new nature. And, with this new nature, we have the opportunity to choose who's voice we will heed.

Rise up, child of God! Don't let your life pass away as you settle for less. Heed the truth and allow God to make you into a person worthy of His image!

TALKING TO THE COACH

Dear Lord,

How majestic You are and how amazing Your creation!

From nothing, You created galaxies too vast to imagine

and too numerous to count.

With amazing precision, You set the universe in motion

and gave each atom a purpose.

So, why do You love people so much?

Why do You love me at all?

You created me for more, but I have chosen less.

You gave me Your image, yet I disfigure it.

Perhaps this is Your most amazing feature:

Your great love for a creature so unworthy.

Lord, I am helpless and hopeless without You.

Help me to heed Your words of grace and truth,

and to rise above the deluding downward drag of sin.

In Jesus' name I pray,

AMEN. AMEN. **AMEN!**

GAME TIME

1. What moral failure seems to have the most power over you?

2. The best—and only—way to answer a lie is with the Truth (i.e. Scripture). How much Truth do you take in compared to the untruth you hear on a daily basis?

3. What are some creative ways you can keep God's Truth handy when ambushed by temptation, negativity, discouragement, or shame? When will you put these creative solutions to work?

CHARACTER REVEALED

THE PLAYBOOK

...Eventually God will bring everything that we do out into the open and judge it according to its hidden intent, whether it's good or evil. (Ecclesiastes 12:14 MSG)

THE GAME PLAN

"Let's take a knee."

You've seen it in the news; another professional athlete is exposed for his hidden lifestyle.

Many star players have distinguished themselves as the best of the best in their respective fields. They played their way into the hearts of fans and the pages of record books. But they also share something else in common. They all believed the same lie. They believed their secret lives had no bearing on their public lives. And they were equally shocked when mistresses betrayed them to tabloids, photos found their way onto the internet, marriages crumbled, and their fans discovered the ugly truth. Where dedication and discipline made these men legends in public, they failed where life counts most: in private.

Reputation is who people say you are. Character is who you really are. According to the Bible, your reputation will, sooner or later, reflect your character. You will eventually become known for who you really are. Count on it. So, rather than waste time trying to maintain a good public image, why not put that energy into building genuine character?

takeakneebook.com

Several years ago, I attended a breakfast for teenagers in Washington, D.C. where five hundred kids crowded into a basketball gym to hear men of renown talk about their relationship with Jesus Christ. When the event ended, the teenagers dashed off to class and the keynote speakers departed for other important meetings. As I stood up to leave, I noticed a man folding and stacking chairs as fast as he could. His shirt sleeves were rolled up, his tie tucked into his shirt, and a sharp-looking suit jacket lay folded on the gym floor.

I nudged the friend who had come with me. "Who's the well-dressed janitor?" I asked.

He answered, "Oh, that's Senator Mark Hatfield."

It was a priceless moment. I watched in silence as a five-term U.S. Senator—a man worthy of his own chapter in Tom Brokaw's book, The Greatest Generation—stacked chairs without a reporter or photographer within a mile. He cared so much for these kids—and for leading them to Christ—that he devoted his morning to a task most men would consider too menial for their stature.

Character isn't revealed in the big moments of glory, but in the decisions we make when we think no one is looking. At these times, we are faced with an opportunity to build genuine character or craft an impressive public relations campaign.

I urge you; be more concerned with your character than your reputation. Eventually, you will be known for your character anyway.

TALKING TO THE COACH

Dear Lord,

Help me to be a person of character,

> *a person with a good heart,*
>
> *a person who is respectful,*
>
> *a person who encourages my teammates,*
>
> *a person who doesn't whine or complain,*
>
> *and a person who doesn't make excuses.*

Teach me to love You and to obey You when no one else notices.

Remind me that each day is a gift and help me to invest it well.

Build me into the kind of person who wins humbly,

> *who learns through disappointment,*
>
> *who takes a loss like a champion.*
>
> *and who never gives up.*

In Jesus' name I pray,

AMEN. AMEN. **AMEN!**

takeakneebook.com

GAME TIME

1. If your life was captured on video, would you feel comfortable doing a screening for your family? Your friends? Why, or why not?

2. Think through any parts of the tape you might want to hide. What do they reveal about your character? Come up with two or three action items to work on these issues. What will you do? When will you do it?

3. Look for opportunities to develop good character—ways to love, care for, or help someone behind the scenes. Make a habit of finding opportunities and then act on them often.

LITTLE BIG THINGS

THE PLAYBOOK

"His master replied, 'Well done, good and faithful servant! You have been faithful with a few things; I will put you in charge of many things. Come and share your master's happiness!'"
(Matthew 25:23 NIV84)

THE GAME PLAN

"Let's take a knee."

When's the last time you thought about the lug nuts on your car? (Didn't expect that question today, did you?) Nine ounces of steel, shaped like a hexagon with a threaded hole in the middle. Not much to look at. Reasonably cheap to buy. Common to everything on the road with four or more wheels. Rarely given a second thought until it's time to change a flat or rotate the tires. Yet think about how important they are. A mere handful keeps a ton of steel and rubber safely rolling down the road at seventy miles per hour. And I don't care what kind of car you drive—whether a $150,000 Italian beauty or a $150 junker—you're going nowhere without the faithful, humble lug nut doing its job.

Sometimes, I feel like a lug nut. I'm willing to bet you do too. As long as you stay screwed down tight, faithfully keeping your part of the world rolling along, others barely notice your presence and rarely appreciate your significance, except maybe on greeting card holidays. But let me assure you, someone very important takes note of your faithfulness and has promised to reward you handsomely. Jesus said those who have been

takeakneebook.com

faithful with a few things will be put in charge of many things, and He always keeps His promises. More than that, He always exceeds expectations.

You may or may not receive the accolades you deserve in this life, but you can be certain of this: we won't be sitting around on clouds, playing harps in the next life. Every indication of Scripture indicates we will have jobs to do and responsibilities to uphold in eternity. This life is merely a job interview, and the chief qualification is faithfulness.

Stay at it. Hear the applause of heaven. "Humble yourselves, therefore, under God's mighty hand, that he may lift you up in due time" (1 Peter 5:6 NIV84), whether in this life or the next.

TALKING TO THE COACH

Dear Lord,
Though the world prizes pretentiousness,
and rewards pride with celebrity,
teach me to seek Your approval
rather than the applause of men.
Remove all need for accolades
leaving only contentment in the knowledge
that You promise to reward faithfulness
and You always pay Your debts.
Give me patience to wait on Your timing
and let me see the future through Your eyes.
If my life is worthy of any glory,
may the glory be Yours and Yours alone.
In Jesus' name I pray,

AMEN. AMEN. **AMEN!**

takeakneebook.com

GAME TIME

1. When do you feel most undervalued or the least appreciated?

2. What role do you think your faith in God plays in your desire for recognition?

3. Read Matthew 18:1-4 and 1 Peter 5:6. What is one specific action you can take during those times to get your mind off yourself and focused on God's priorities? Share your thoughts with someone close and ask for his help during those difficult times.

THINKING SUCCESS

THE PLAYBOOK

Brothers and sisters, whatever is true, whatever is noble, whatever is right, whatever is pure, whatever is lovely, whatever is admirable—if anything is excellent or praiseworthy—think about such things. (Philippians 4:8 NIV84)

THE GAME PLAN

"Let's take a knee."

An old man's faithful sidekick, Blue, finally died after many seasons of hunting together. It can take years to train a dog to retrieve ducks without either eating them or mauling them to pieces, so the old gentleman was amazed to find a new hunting dog that not only retrieved on command, but literally walked on water. He couldn't wait to show his friend, Pete.

The following week, the old man and Pete sat in their duck blind, and as the birds flew across the water, they started shooting. The new hunting dog leaped onto the water, scampered across the surface, and returned with a duck. All morning long, the dog ran back and forth across the water, retrieving fallen ducks and laying them at the old man's feet.

Finally, the man said to his friend, "Pete, you haven't said a single word about my new huntin' dog."

Pete replied, "He retrieves just fine, but he ain't much of a swimmer, is he?"

Some people have the uncanny ability to see the dark

side of everything. Others somehow manage to find potential good in any circumstance. I don't know about you, but I know which kind of person I like to be around more!

Thinking good thoughts usually produces good results. That doesn't mean you have to live in denial; it merely means you choose to emphasize the potential good in any circumstance rather than focus on the drawbacks. In fact, some of the world's greatest success stories begin with failure and some of the most amazing technological advances emerged from failed experiments.

I wonder how many more success stories we'd hear if more people saw problems as opportunities in disguise.

TALKING TO THE COACH

Dear Lord,

The world is negative enough without negative people.

You have given me every reason for optimism,

despite the evil I see at work all around,

Your will and Your people will prevail.

Therefore, give me a winning attitude.

Show me the positive potential in every circumstance,

train my mind to focus on the good,

and may I be the first to show it to others.

In Jesus' name I pray,

AMEN. **AMEN. AMEN!**

takeakneebook.com

GAME TIME

1. Think about the week you've just finished. Identify one situation that most would consider negative.

2. With that situation in mind, what potential good might be found in it when you view it with a positive perspective?

3. How can you help others see the good and how might you seize the opportunity to turn this into a success? Think of a way to remember this when a negative situation needs some positive thinking.

SUCCESS IN SIGHT

THE PLAYBOOK

We have not received the spirit of the world but the Spirit who is from God, that we may understand what God has freely given us. This is what we speak, not in words taught us by human wisdom but in words taught by the Spirit, expressing spiritual truths in spiritual words. "For who has known the mind of the Lord that he may instruct him?" But we have the mind of Christ.
(1 Corinthians 2:12–13, 16 NIV84)

THE GAME PLAN

"Let's take a knee."

There's a huge difference between winning and not losing, between succeeding and not failing.

Only an incompetent coach would say to his players, "Don't flub the pass" or "Don't strike out" or "Don't air-ball the free throw." That's because our brains are wired to learn what to do rather than what not to do. The vast majority of the human brain is devoted to unconscious learning, which is programmed through effort and experience, trial and success. We learn best through positive experience and reinforcement.

Trying to train the mind from a negative perspective, however, is like trying to drive a car by watching the rearview mirror only. You would never learn how to avoid accidents, only how to recover from them. After a few wrecks, walking looks a lot more pleasant—and safer!

Programming the positive is a simple switch. Rather than focusing on what not to do, we must face forward, anticipating what we can do and then choosing accordingly. Successful quarterbacks learn to see themselves throwing a perfectly timed spiral into the receiver's hands. Batters learn to see themselves watching the pitch and then swinging through the baseball. Basketball players often envision the free throw just before shooting. They see success in their minds and then follow through with their bodies.

Follow their example. See yourself performing well on the job. Imagine yourself listening to your spouse, playing with your children, supporting a friend, or greeting a stranger. Hear yourself saying good words. See yourself growing deeper in your faith. Feel respect strengthening within you and radiating outward to others.

See it. Then *do it*.

TALKING TO THE COACH

Dear Lord,

Thank You for the gift of Your Spirit,

through whom Your will becomes attainable

and with whom all good deeds are possible.

Thank You for wanting what's best for me,

and for giving me what I need rather than what I want.

Thank You for giving me the mind of Your Son,

so that His desires become my desires.

Teach me to envision His example,

to see myself following His model,

and then pleasing You through my actions.

In Jesus' name I pray,

AMEN. AMEN. **AMEN!**

GAME TIME

1. Read Colossians 3:23. What praiseworthy activity would you like to do "with excellence"? Choose one for now and make it your prayer focus for the next week.

2. Using your calendar, decide when you will devote fifteen minutes each day to quiet solitude in order to focus your thoughts on the Lord and talk through this activity with Him. How will He be honored in this activity?

3. Set that time aside as a regular appointment and protect it. Devote fifteen minutes each day, for one week, to envisioning yourself fulfilling that activity with excellence.

THE POSSIBLE DREAM

THE PLAYBOOK

...Seek first his kingdom and his righteousness, and all these things will be given to you as well. (Matthew 6:33 NIV84)

THE GAME PLAN

"Let's take a knee."

The title, "World's Fastest Human," was first used in the 1920s to describe Olympic runner, Charlie Paddock, who dominated the 100-meter race for many years. In 1932, he visited a group of high school students in Cleveland, Ohio, where a young man decided he wanted the title for himself. "J.C." shared his dream with his track coach, Charles Riley, who encouraged the sprinter to add three words to his vocabulary and to build every aspect of his life around them: determination, dedication, and discipline.

Determination – Don't let anything deter you from reaching your goal.

Dedication – Don't let anything dissuade you from reaching your goal.

Discipline – Don't let anything distract you from reaching your goal.

"J.C." kicked his training into high gear and later that year beat Paddock's old 100-meter record by a full second. The following year, as a high school senior, he

takeakneebook.com

tied the existing world record. In 1934, he attended Ohio State University, where as a black athlete, he had to live off-campus, stay at black-only hotels and eat at black-only restaurants on road trips, received no scholarship like his slower teammates, and worked to pay his way through school. Still, he set three world records and tied a fourth at a single meet. And in 1936, the man known to the world as Jesse Owens traveled to Nazi Germany, where he won four Olympic gold medals (100-meters, 200-meters, Long Jump, and 4 x 100 Relay), a feat not equaled until 1984.

What is your dream? Has it occurred to you that the Lord may have given you that dream? Have you stopped to think He wants you to achieve your dream and He's waiting for you to accomplish it His way? I want to challenge you to submit your dream to God. Rather than achieve it all on your own, let Him bring it to fulfillment through you. That doesn't take away from Coach Riley's advice. Make the three words—*determination, dedication, and discipline*—primary in your vocabulary and in your daily activities. Then add a fourth to rule the other three and to become your supreme guide: *Surrender*.

God's kingdom and His righteousness have plenty of room in them for your dream. It's just a matter of priority. Surrender your dream to God's will, to be accomplished His way, then give it your all!

TALKING TO THE COACH

Dear Lord,
I have visions of the future
that may or may not be pleasing to You.
Where my desires displease You,
forgive me, transform my mind,
replace my foolishness with Your wisdom.
Where my dreams are pleasing to You,
I give thanks for these gifts,
and I submit them to Your control.
As I seek Your kingdom, and Your right living,
bring my honorable desires to fulfillment,
for my joy and to Your glory.
In Jesus' name I pray,

AMEN. **AMEN.** **AMEN!**

GAME TIME

1. Do you have a dream? If you do not have a Christ-centered vision for your future, ask the Lord to give you one!

2. If you do have a dream you would like to fulfill, surrender it to the Lord now, completely and without reservation.

3. Include in your daily prayer a request similar to this: "Lord, show me what I should do today to fulfill the dream You have destined me to accomplish."

A MAN'S GOT TO KNOW HIS LIMITATIONS

THE PLAYBOOK

As iron sharpens iron, so one man sharpens another. (Proverbs 27:17 NIV84)

THE GAME PLAN

"Let's take a knee."

Years ago, I lived next door to Robin Parkhouse, who played football under Bear Bryant. The legendary coach once called Robin the toughest lineman he ever coached at Alabama, and I can believe it. Robin Parkhouse was an animal on the field, and not much more civilized in life. He once said, "I wasn't the one who necessarily would start the trouble, but I was always available for trouble." And it had a way of finding him often. Enough to land him in jail, where reading the Gospel of John convinced Robin to ask Jesus Christ for help. His life was powerfully transformed on that day.

According to Robin, Coach Bryant approached life like he did football. On several occasions, both on and off the field, Bear would say, "Suck up your guts and keep going. Suck it up!" And that's pretty good advice in a lot of instances. When things aren't going well in your marriage, your career, or life in general, you just need to suck it up and keep doing what you should be doing. Just like in athletic competition, sometimes you have to play hurt, you have to keep going through the pain.

takeakneebook.com

There's a terrible downside to that advice, though. Sometimes, you simply can't suck up your guts and keep going. Sometimes, you need a close buddy or somebody you can trust to whom you can say, "You know, man, I'm suckin' wind. I'm hurtin'. I'm scared. I've screwed up. I can't do this on my own. I need help." In my experience, it's stupid to keep doing what *doesn't work*, and there comes a time when a man has to stop trying to gut his way through life.

God expects us to be men; He never created us to be *supermen*. That's why He encourages us to band together for continuing development, for mutual support, and for trustworthy advice. I'm convinced everyone needs a mentor to help keep his head screwed on straight and a handful of peers to offer the occasional swift kick in the rear. I've seen lots of athletic careers in my service to professional teams. The players who made it far, never got there alone.

TALKING TO THE COACH

Dear Lord,

Thank You for making me determined and resilient,

a person who doesn't look for excuses or easy outs.

Make me even stronger and fill me with courage.

Inspire me to do what is right when no one else will.

Give me the ability to rise above adversity

and to press on through difficulty.

But, Lord, give me the good sense to ask for help.

Forgive my stubborn independence,

and replace my foolish self-sufficiency

with the wisdom to join forces with other children of God.

In Jesus' name I pray,

AMEN. AMEN. **AMEN!**

GAME TIME

1. When is it wise to just "suck it up" and keep going?

2. When is it just plain stupid to not seek the help of trustworthy friends?

3. If you don't have someone in your life who can help you see the difference when you've lost perspective, seek one out. Begin immediately to cultivate this kind of relationship.

HONING YOUR COMPETITIVE EDGE

THE PLAYBOOK

Let the wise listen and add to their learning, and let the discerning get guidance—for understanding proverbs and parables, the sayings and riddles of the wise. The fear of the LORD is the beginning of knowledge, but fools despise wisdom and discipline. (Proverbs 1:5–7 NIV84)

THE GAME PLAN

"Let's take a knee."

I like working with men, but sometimes they drive me a little crazy. God gave men an independent streak that gets the job done in spite of hardships, but that same independent mindset can also get in the way of good sense. Some guys think that asking a more experienced man to become a mentor is either beneath their dignity or undermines the respect of their peers. They also avoid banding together with other men for fear of losing their competitive edge. That's not only proof of the worst kind of pride, *it's just not true!*

Years ago, when I started as a chaplain for the National Basketball Association, I began in Houston with the Rockets. I didn't know any better, I guess, so I used to bring both competing teams together before the game. Forty-five minutes before tipoff, before either team warmed up, we'd gather in one room. There was Julius Irving and Bobby Jones to the right. There was Rick Berry and Robert Reid to the left. Everybody having a little study, locking arms, and praying. Then they'd go out on the floor and kill each other. After meeting together around Christ, gaining greater respect for one another, they competed harder than ever. Far from diminishing their competitive nature, their mutual respect brought out their best. And, man, *they got after it.*

That's when I really enjoy my job. I love seeing Jesus Christ, in men, bringing out the best in other men. When that happens, they become well-rounded individuals, focused on four basic priorities:

- their commitment to Jesus Christ

- their commitment to personal development

- their commitment to healthy relationships

- their commitment to improving the world.

If you're a lone ranger, then get used to the bottom of the heap. If, on the other hand, you're meaningfully involved in the lives of other men, then you have seized an incredible opportunity that can't be described, only experienced. If you're on the receiving end of another man's wisdom and experience, you now enjoy an invaluable resource. Congratulations! You will go far, and I will want to learn from you.

TALKING TO THE COACH

Dear Lord,

Destroy the pride within me that keeps me isolated,

and cultivate within me a hunger for practical wisdom.

The people who listen to Your counsel

are the people I want to emulate.

They have their priorities clearly established by You,

and their insights offer guidance I cannot afford to miss.

So, lead me to where spiritual understanding lives;

and surround me with people of good judgment.

Then, as I receive this heritage of practical wisdom,

may I become a worthy guide to the next generation.

In Jesus' name I pray,

AMEN. AMEN. **AMEN!**

takeakneebook.com

GAME TIME

1. Who is (or was) your strongest, most constructive person of influence, and how did he impact your understanding of the world, yourself, and your purpose?

2. If you haven't had a good mentor, think of an older person you respect, schedule a time to meet informally, and ask his advice on some topic. Then, ask that person to meet you again the next week. If his counsel is godly wisdom, consider asking him to mentor you on a regular basis.[7]

3. Who do you think might look up to you? How can you pass along the lessons you have learned? Pray. Plan a time to meet with him and ask him how he's doing. Listen to the Lord for how to respond.

---

7 For appropriate mentor relationships, men should seek out other men and women should seek out women. The Four Priorities by Dr. John Tolson and Larry Kreider is an excellent resource for mentors. Visit thetolsongroup.com for more information."

APPENDIX:
How to Get to Heaven in Four Downs

Ever wonder why you need Jesus?

The Bible states that, in the beginning, God made humanity flawless. The first people were morally perfect, living in complete harmony with God and the rest of creation.

But God didn't *force* them into obedience. He gave them the gift of autonomy, self-determination, the privilege of making choices and the dignity of living by the consequences of those choices. The first people,

Adam and Eve, were free to either obey God or disobey Him. He said, "You are free to eat from any tree in the garden; but you must not eat from the tree of the knowledge of good and evil, for when you eat of it you will surely die" (Genesis 2:16–17 NIV84). After all, God didn't want the love of robots; He created people to enjoy a relationship based on freely-given love and complete trust in Him.

The first people obeyed for a time, and then did the unthinkable. They chose to disobey. They chose to go their own way rather than live God's way. And in their disobedience and defiance they brought upon the world four lingering consequences that impacted them, and continue to impact us today.

First, we are cut off from God.

Our relationship with Him is broken, and we are spiritually disconnected from Him. When I unplug a lamp, the light goes out. The same has happened to us. We are cut off from the One who made us, gives us life, provides for our needs, and gives us purpose. We might fill our lives with things to make us feel alive, feel meaningful, or feel hopeful, but nothing will ever replace what we're missing from the Life-giver.

takeakneebook.com

Second, we are cut off from ourselves.

There's nobody on the planet who has it all together. Emotionally. Psychologically. Mentally. Physically. All of us are born imperfect... *out-of-whack* in some ways. All of us have wounds and deficiencies that go back further than we can remember. When a man is unplugged from God, it has a devastating effect on how he views himself. The same is true of a woman. And our society bears that out as we see people desperately searching for purpose and significance. This futile search for significance has spawned an endless variety of vices, addictions, psychological problems, and coping mechanisms.

Third, we are cut off from each other.

Soon after the first man and woman disobeyed God, they started pointing the finger at one another, and we've been throwing each other under the bus ever since. The national divorce rate is nearly fifty percent. In West Palm Beach County, Florida, where I spoke recently, I was told that 62.1% of all marriages end in divorce. People don't live in peace, so we have police, attorneys, judges, and jails to contain crime. People don't keep their word, so we have a civil code that takes people years to understand. The world is now defined by conflict.

Fourth, everything in the created world has been affected.

To put it simply, there's something terribly wrong with everything. Nothing in the world remains unaffected by the evil that was first introduced through one disobedient act. So there are natural disasters and deadly diseases. Each of us continues to make the problem of evil worse by adding our own wrongdoings to the chaos. All of us are guilty; none of us can claim moral perfection. All we can do is point to the next guy and try to prove that his sins are worse than our own.

According to the Bible, God is one-hundred-percent perfect, and He will tolerate nothing less than one hundred percent moral perfection in His presence. To violate any portion of His moral code is to reject Him personally. Deep in the core of His nature is justice, so all wrongdoing must be punished. So, even the most moral person in the world cannot meet God's standard of goodness if he or she bears the guilt of just one, single, solitary sin.

takeakneebook.com

That's the bad news. We are hopelessly lost if the task of restoring the relationship is our responsibility.

Fortunately, there's good news. To put it in football terms, if the *goal line* is a restored relationship with God, then are there four "downs" we must consider in order to get there:

1ST DOWN:
GOD LOOKED
DOWN. *John 3:16-17*

The Lord could have said, "Well, you blew it. You had your chance. I gave you everything you needed to be happy, healthy, whole, and fulfilled, but you had to do it your own way. You made this mess, now live with it. In fact, the just penalty of your rebellion is death (Romans 6:23), so I'm going to let justice take its course."

But He didn't say that. Instead, "God so loved the world that He gave His one and only Son so that whoever believes in Him shall not perish, but have eternal life" (John 3:16 NIV84). He didn't love what people did to disconnect themselves from Him, but He loved people. He loved us and had compassion for us. But He didn't stop there.

2ND DOWN: JESUS CAME DOWN.

Jesus +

Philippians 2:5-7

While God hates evil, He loves people. But that causes a dilemma. You see, the problem isn't merely the bad things we have done; we are infected with a moral cancer called "sin." And until the disease of sin is eradicated from within, we cannot avoid future wrongdoing. That's why willpower is never enough. As hard as you try, you cannot keep from sinning because you are sinful all the way down to your DNA. Consequently, it's going to take something miraculous to cure us of this moral disease.

The cure came to earth when God became a man in the person of Jesus Christ. *Fully human*, so He could represent us. *Morally perfect*, so He was qualified to bear the penalty of others. And *fully God*, so that He could not only die the death owed by all people, but rise again to conquer death and live on. Jesus Christ, God in human flesh, was born and then lived as people ought to live. And for thirty-plus years, He lived an incredible life. When He spoke, people listened. When He touched people, their diseases were healed. When

takeakneebook.com

He confronted evil, it shrank from His presence. But through it all, He knew He had a mission.

3RD DOWN: JESUS CHRIST LAID DOWN. *Philippians 2:8*

In Romans 6:23 we learn that "The wages of sin is death, but the gift of God is eternal life in Christ Jesus our Lord." Jesus Christ came to earth to become our substitute, to pay the penalty of death that we owe for all the bad things we have done. He came as the perfect representation of good on earth, which drew the wrath of evil. As Jesus, Himself, stated, "Light has come into the world, but men loved darkness instead of light because their deeds were evil" (John 3:19 NIV84). Rather than accept Jesus as their king, evil people rejected Him, beat Him to a bloody pulp, and executed Him on a cross to get rid of Him.

Evil put the Son of God down, but He didn't stay down. Evil put Jesus to death, but He didn't stay dead. Having paid the penalty of sin on behalf of all people, He rose from the dead—literally, not just figuratively or spiritually. He left behind an empty tomb, having risen to a new kind of life. And now He offers this new kind of life to all who will receive His gift.

4TH DOWN: EVERY KNEE MUST BOW DOWN. *Philippians 2:9-11*

From the beginning, God said that the just penalty for rebelling against Him is death (Genesis 2:16–17; Romans 6:23). Not just the demise of the physical body, but spiritual death (Revelation 20:14–15), which is eternal torment in hell. That's not a pleasant thought, but it is nonetheless true. While Jesus bore the penalty on behalf of all humanity, He didn't set aside the gift of autonomy originally given to people back in Genesis. We are not automatically saved from sin whether we want it or not. We still possess the gift of choice and the dignity of living with the consequences of our choices. And so it is with the gift of Jesus Christ's death on our behalf.

The penalty of sin is death, and you have a choice as to how that debt will be paid. You can reject Jesus Christ's sacrificial gift and pay it yourself by choosing hell, or you can let His death satisfy your debt.

To accept His gift, you merely admit you cannot overcome the internal problem of evil on your own. You admit you are powerless to save yourself or even clean up your own act. And in that realization of helplessness, you ask for Christ to accomplish for you, and within you, what you cannot do yourself. You say, "Lord, I bow down. I give You everything. I want You to come into my life, rid me of the disease of sin, clean up my mess, make me the person You created me to be, and someday welcome me into Your eternal presence when my physical life ends."

If you're at the place right now where you would like to bow your knee and accept this gift of healing from the disease of sin and receive the promise of eternal life, you simply pray something like the following. This is just an example prayer; there are no magic words. This is not about saying or doing the right thing. All you're doing is admitting you need God to save you, believing His promise to welcome you, and accepting His free gift of Himself in your life.

> *Dear God,*
>
> *I admit that I am helpless to overcome my shortcomings to be the person You want me to be. I also admit that the things I have*

done and the disease of sin within me has disconnected me from You, and that I deserve eternal death as a penalty for my sin. Thank You for sending Your Son, Jesus, to die in my place.

Jesus, please come into my life right now! I trust in You alone to pay the penalty of my sins and to grant me forgiveness. I accept Your gift of eternal life, and I ask You to be the Lord of my life. Thank You.

In Jesus' name,

Amen.

If that prayer expresses your thoughts, then you have received a wonderful gift! *Your life will never be the same.* Moreover, you have joined an extended family of believers. So, let me be the first to say, "Welcome to the family of God!"

So, how can you be sure Jesus came into your life? Read John 1:12 and 1 John 5:11-13 for the answer. Did you receive Him? Do you believe in Jesus? If you received Jesus and you believe in Him, then according to God's Word, Jesus is in your life! God cannot lie (Titus 1:2) and if He says it, we can believe it!

APPENDIX

P.S. You have begun a new journey, but you don't have to walk alone. You have many friends who would count it a privilege to help you know what comes next. I would love to hear from you and help put you in touch with other men who have walked the path you have begun. Please contact me at john@thetolsongroup.com.

CHALLENGE
BY ROGER STAUBACH

Take a Knee is a good start. As you have discovered, John has written down thirty-one days of practical lessons from Scripture. Each carefully chosen topic addresses the heart of man. *Pride and humility. Work and laziness. Integrity and hypocrisy. Diligence and negligence. Faithfulness and cowardice.* Each daily message, when studied and applied, will help you build strength in a particular area of Christian character. Like a well-planned weight training program, followed consistently and conscientiously, Take a Knee will help you cultivate an authentic relationship with God, who will then build your Christian strength from the inside out.

In fact, Take a Knee could become a simple way for us, as men, to become the spiritual leaders God has called us to be. Imagine the impact you could have in helping shape the character of your children. Imagine how our nation and culture could be transformed as fathers invest in the personal development of their children. Imagine this becoming a movement, beginning with the simple decision to use the book you hold in your hands as a discussion-starter with your kids.

I plan to use Take a Knee with my grandchildren. I'm looking forward to seeing how our relationships will grow closer. I trust that the gift of my time and the practicality of these lessons will help them establish strong habits early. I expect that our time together will help prepare them for success, not only spiritually, but in every arena of life.

> **"Take a Knee will help you cultivate an authentic relationship with God, who will then build your Christian strength from the inside out."**

My challenge to you is to do the same! Read Take a Knee with your children and grandchildren daily. Talk about the challenge for each day and find ways to act on it at school, work, or in your neighborhood. Regroup and talk about your experiences, then begin again with the next day. Are you up for the challenge?

Roger Staubach
Former NFL quarterback and two-time Super Bowl champion for the Dallas Cowboys

ABOUT THE AUTHOR

Dr. John Tolson is a nationally renowned teacher, speaker and author who, for more than 30 years, has spiritually mentored hundreds and thousands of adults and students – in fact, about one million have been helped through The Gathering, a discipleship ministry he founded. John's deepest desire is to see people become the leaders God created them to be: successful in family, life, & business.

> **"Achieving balance in all things is the truest measure of success. It's not letting what you don't do well interfere with what you do best."**
> **—Dr. John Tolson**

John serves as a spiritual life coach for some of the nation's leading executives, celebrities, and athletes. He started one of the first team chaplain programs in the NBA, and he has served professional teams including the Houston Rockets, Houston Astros, Houston Oilers, Orlando Magic and most recently, the Dallas Cowboys.

takeakneebook.com

ABOUT THE AUTHOR

As an avid basketball player and fan – he holds a personal best record of 127 straight free throws.

Dr. Tolson inspires audiences through his global speaking; he's called upon by major corporations including Walt Disney World and Hyatt to keynote conferences and seminars. He is the author of *Take a Knee,* a motivational book based on the locker room messages he gave to the Dallas Cowboys, and co-author of *The Four Priorities,* which challenges men and women to mature in their faith. Married to Punky Leonard Tolson since 2001, John is the father of two grown children with his late wife Ruth Anne, and has three adorable grandchildren.

Thank you for purchasing Take a Knee by Dr. John Tolson!

To schedule John for your next corporate or ministry event, please contact our ministry office at info@thetolsongroup.com.